Misterio

Manu, detective

Lista de honor Premio CCEI 2008

Pilar Lozano Carbayo

Ilustración
Francesc Rovira

Taller de lectura
Begoña Lozano y Alfredo Borque

© Pilar Lozano Carbayo.
© Grupo Editorial Bruño, S. L., 2007.
Juan Ignacio Luca de Tena, 15. 28027 Madrid.
www.brunolibros.es

Dirección del proyecto editorial
Trini Marull

Dirección editorial
Isabel Carril

Edición
Begoña Lozano

Preimpresión
Luis Alberto García

Diseño
Inventa Comunicación

Este libro dispone de un **cuaderno de Lectura Eficaz.**

Primera edición: febrero 2007
Decimosexta edición: septiembre 2019

Reservados todos los derechos. Quedan rigurosamente
prohibidas, sin el permiso escrito de los titulares
del *copyright*, la reproducción o la transmisión total
o parcial de esta obra por cualquier procedimiento
mecánico o electrónico, incluyendo la reprografía
y el tratamiento informático, y la distribución
de ejemplares mediante alquiler o préstamo públicos.

Pueden utilizarse citas siempre que se mencione
su procedencia.

ISBN: 978-84-216-9862-4
D. legal: M-11418-2011

Printed in Spain

PAPEL DE FIBRA
CERTIFICADO

Pilar Lozano Carbayo

La autora

- Me gustan las palabras muchísimo. Escribirlas, pronunciarlas, averiguar su significado, leerlas, jugar con ellas, inventar relatos…; por eso elegí como profesión el periodismo y como afición la literatura.

- Crecí en una familia de diez hermanos. Y fue divertido ser niña. Tanto, que de vez en cuando me gusta volver a la infancia y vivir y jugar con los personajes que me invento.

- He ganado varios premios: el Premio de Literatura Infantil Barco de Vapor con *Siete reporteros y un periódico;* el Premio Edebé con *¡No es tan fácil ser niño!,* y el Premio Lazarillo con *Marco Polo no fue solo.*

Para ti...

¡Me encanta Manu! Es un niño normal, divertido, bueno, alegre... Pero no, no es solo eso; lo que más me gusta de Manu es que es ¡superpositivo!

Siempre ve el lado bueno de las cosas; por eso, además de un buen detective, ¡está destinado a ser feliz! Y eso es muy contagioso.

Yo me lo he pasado muy bien escribiendo esta aventura de Manu. Y el dibujante ¡se lo pasó en grande y le salieron unos dibujos preciosos! También Begoña, la editora, se ha divertido mucho...

Así que ahora te toca a ti disfrutar con Manu. Abre el libro, síguele de cerca en su investigación y verás lo bien que te lo pasas con él y sus amigos...

*A Carlos, Álvaro, Pablo, María, Marta, Ana, Manu, Poli, Javi,
Chari, mamá, Cita y Proco, Begoña y Alfredo,
Suca y Ramón, Teresa y Fernando, Rafa y Marisa,
Fina y Chema, Josema y Maica, Jano y Yolanda,
Jandri y Maite, José Luis y Gloria, Antonio y María Paz...,
todos los que estuvieron allí con sus cariños y sus risas.
A Javier y María José, que rondaron por allí.
Y a Nuria, Jorge, Jesús y Esperanza, Juan Luis y Emilia,
Rafa y Paquita, Yoyi, Miguel, Diana, José, Montse y Elena,
que les hubiera gustado estar allí.
«Allí» es un inolvidable fin de semana en Arredondo.
A todos, gracias.*

1

Una tarjeta falsa

—ES falsa –dije. Y tiré la tarjeta con desprecio sobre la mesa.

Ana cambió la expresión de su cara, pasando de una sonrisa orgullosa a una mueca de pena. Y de la pena, a unos pucheros, y de los pucheros, al lloriqueo.

Vamos, que yo, sin quererlo, la había liado.

Entre sollozos, Ana me contó que era la primera tarjeta de invitación a un cumpleaños que había recibido en su vida y que estaba muy ilusionada.

Pero claro, si era falsa... «¿Por qué? ¿Por qué?», se preguntaba.

Para consolarla, pensé que lo mejor era averiguar qué había detrás de aquella extraña tarjeta. Y entonces fue cuando decidí hacerme detective. Así, sobre la marcha.

—Ana, si quieres, puedo investigar quién te la ha mandado y con qué intenciones... ¿Sabes?, puedo ser tu detective... –añadí yo para animarla.

Ana dejó repentinamente de llorar. Se levantó muy enfadada y con determinación me dijo:

—No necesito detectives. Ya me imagino quién me la ha enviado. Seguro que ha sido el cerdo de Pablo, que siempre quiere chincharme.
Pues se va a enterar.

Cogió la tarjeta y salió dando un portazo.

Me quedé solo en la clase acabando la pintura de un mural sobre

«Cómo es tu barrio», que nos habían
encargado para la fiesta
de la primavera.

Estaba ensimismado en la tarea
de pintar cada casa de un color
distinto, más que nada para animar
el barrio, que en la realidad tiene todas
las casas de ladrillo y resulta un poco
aburrido.

O sea, que ya ni me acordaba
de Ana ni de su tarjeta de cumpleaños
cuando, de repente, se abrió
la puerta y entró acompañada de Pablo,
que chillaba como un loco:

—¡Suéltame! ¡Yo no he sido!

Ana le empujó hasta sentarle sobre
una silla a mi lado, y continuó tirándole
de la oreja. Muy seria, me dijo:

—Interrógale.

Y a modo de explicación le informó a Pablo:

—Que sepas que Manu es detective.

Pablo y yo nos miramos a cuál más sorprendido.

2

Primer sospechoso

—**S**UÉLTALE. Yo no interrogo bajo torturas –dije muy serio.

Pensaba que como detective debía imponer mi autoridad. Me levanté de mi asiento y empecé a dar vueltas alrededor de Pablo, con las manos a mi espalda, haciéndome el interesante. Vamos, como un auténtico detective.

—Verás lo que ha acontecido –le dije finalmente.

—¿Acontecido? –dijo Pablo, que al parecer llevaba un rato sin entender nada.

—Sí, Pablo, he dicho «ha acontecido»,
que quiere decir «ha pasado».
Y no interrumpas.

Y seguí contándole:

—Pues resulta que Ana ha encontrado
esta mañana encima de su pupitre
una tarjeta de invitación para una fiesta
de cumpleaños en la que no pone
ni quién cumple años, ni dónde
se celebra. Yo la he examinado
con atención y he llegado
a una conclusión evidente:
esa tarjeta es falsa.

Me volví hacia Ana y le dije:

—Por favor, enseña la tarjeta
al sospechoso.

Ana, siguiendo las instrucciones
de su detective, se la entregó
de inmediato.

—Pablo, ¿reconoces esta tarjeta?
–le pregunté.

Pablo la miró por delante
y por detrás, y la leyó en voz alta:

—«Estás invitada a mi cumpleaños.
No faltes».

Le dio la vuelta y leyó la firma:

—«La mano negra,
el gorro rojo,
yo hago siempre
lo que es mi antojo».

Y en ese momento, Pablo exclamó:

—¡Guau! ¡Cómo mola!
¡Yo no he escrito esto, de verdad!
¡Pero si a mí no se me hubiera
ocurrido eso tan molón! Y además
–añadió con envidia–, yo no
sé dibujar tan bien.

Y es que Pablo tenía razón. La tarjeta
molaba. Por la parte de delante
llevaba una tarta de tres pisos,
cada uno de un color.
Y encima, unas velas preciosas.
Por detrás, esa poesía tan estupenda,
que la verdad es que a mí también
me encantaba.

Pero no me entretuve en exclamaciones
y seguí con mi interrogatorio.

—¿Se le ocurre al sospechoso
quién puede haber sido el autor?

—No tengo ni idea, y además, Manu,
¡que yo no soy sospechoso!
Pero lo que SÍ puedo ser,
y me encantaría, es tu ayudante.
Me haré una tarjeta
de presentación:

> **PABLO MORENO**
>
> **Ayudante de detective**

No me dio tiempo a contestarle,
porque Ana, más rápida que yo,
que las niñas parece que están siempre
más al loro, le dijo que desde luego
a él no pensaba pagarle ni un céntimo
por sus investigaciones.

—¿Y a mí sí? –le pregunté yo muy animado, que hasta ese momento ni se me había pasado por la imaginación que pudiera llegar a cobrar por ser detective.

—Si descubres quién ha sido, sí. A ti te pagaré.

—Y ¿cuánto?

Ana se quedó pensativa y finalmente me dijo que me regalaría alguno de los juguetes de su hermano, que tenía tantos que ni se iba a enterar.

—¿Qué tal una bici? –le propuse.

Me miró abriendo mucho los ojos, con un gesto de «pero bueno, ¿tú qué te has creído?», y ni me contestó.

—Y si la bici es pequeña... –dije yo, intentando arreglarlo.

—Tú estás loco.

—¿Y qué tal un casco para montar en bici?

—Bueno, eso sí.

—Acepto –dije yo rápidamente.

La ilusión de mi vida era tener una bicicleta, así que aunque solo me regalara un casco, por algo se empezaba. No podía despreciar esa oportunidad.

—Y tú, Pablo, si quieres, puedes ser mi ayudante. Como pago a tus trabajos te montaré en mi bici.

—Vale –dijo Pablo.

Y es que Pablo, por mucho que dijera Ana que era un cerdo, es muy bueno. Se conformaba tan solo con dar una vuelta en bici, y eso que, de momento, lo único que teníamos era ¡una promesa de casco!

¿Cuántos casos teníamos que resolver para ganar la bicicleta? A lo mejor, nunca la conseguiríamos.

Me encantaba el entusiasmo de mi ayudante.

Un verdadero caso de detective

AL llegar a casa le pregunté a mi padre, que es un gran lector de novelas de detectives, en qué consistía exactamente ese oficio.

—El detective se encarga de buscar al criminal que ha cometido un delito: robos, asesinatos, estafas...; vamos, que busca al malo. Y cuando lo atrapa, lo entrega a la policía, y la policía lo lleva al juzgado y ahí se acaba la novela.

—Eso en las novelas... ¿y en la realidad?

—Pues en la realidad también
busca al malo, pero no siempre
lo encuentra, supongo.

Estaba claro que eso iba
a ser yo: un detective real,
no como los de las novelas.
Vamos, que me podía equivocar
y no resolver nunca el caso
que me había encargado Ana.

Me sentí un poco agobiado,
pero pensé en el casco que
me había prometido y me animé.
Empezaría cuanto antes
mi investigación, aunque
no tenía ni idea de cómo hacerlo.
Realmente iba a necesitar más ayuda
que la de mi amigo Pablo.

Estábamos cenando toda la familia
con el barullo de siempre
–somos cinco hermanos,
mi padre, mi madre y uno de

mis abuelos–, cuando les informé
de que me había hecho detective
y ya tenía un caso que resolver.

Con tanta gente es bastante
difícil que te escuchen, pero
esa vez lo conseguí, aunque para
ello tuve que ponerme encima
de la silla y pedir atención a gritos.

Pensaron que me había vuelto loco
y se quedaron todos mirándome
en silencio. Entonces me senté
y me puse a hablar.

Les dije que necesitaba
ideas para empezar
a investigar.
Les enseñé
también la tarjeta
de invitación.

Empezamos entonces una
conversación muy animada.

Nadie sabía qué significaba aquello
de la mano negra y el gorro rojo,
pero decían que eran pistas que había
que tener en cuenta. Desde luego,
en mi clase, nadie tenía una mano
negra ni un gorro rojo.

—Nos enfrentamos a un caso
un poco complicado –dijo mi padre–,
porque está claro que el autor
no quiere que le descubran.
Por eso no escribe con su letra
y ha compuesto las frases con letras
recortadas de periódicos.

«¡Ahí va! ¡Es verdad! –pensé–.
¡Y yo que creía que lo había hecho así
para que quedara más bonito!».

—O sea, ¡que es un verdadero caso
de detective! –dije yo, emocionado.

Y contagié a la familia mi entusiasmo.
Todos empezaron a dar su opinión

a la vez y a gritos, que es como se
habla en mi casa cuando estamos
todos juntos.

Bueno, el caso es que al final
la tarjeta acabó en la papilla de Elena,
que es mi hermana más pequeña
y es un poco trasto. Y de todas
las cosas que dijeron y pude entender,
saqué una conclusión: para empezar
a investigar tenía que pedirle
a Ana que me hiciera una lista
de sospechosos entre
sus posibles enemigos.

Me pareció una buena idea y confié
en que Ana tuviera algún enemigo.

Sequé la tarjeta con la servilleta
y me fui a dormir.

Mis hermanos mayores todavía
se quedaron discutiendo.

Marta estaba diciendo que
le parecía que la tarjeta no era falsa,
sino que sencillamente
se habían olvidado de firmarla.

Sabré yo, que soy el detective,
si era falsa o no, y además, ¡qué falta
de sensibilidad la de mi hermana!
Si no fuera falsa, ¿cómo se supone
que iba yo a ganar el casco para
la bicicleta?

4

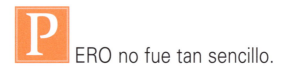

¡Otra tarjeta!

PERO no fue tan sencillo.

Al día siguiente, antes de que
empezara la primera clase,
Pablo se acercó muy nervioso
a mi pupitre y me dijo:

—Mira, Manu, mira lo que me
he encontrado en mi mesa.

Abrí el sobre que me entregaba
y me quedé de piedra.

¡Otra tarjeta! Y también venía firmada
como os podéis imaginar. Así:

Pero había algo muy diferente en esa tarjeta. No había tarta ni invitación. Solo decía:

> PABlo: DEJa A IreNE en paZ y NO VUELVas a ACOMPAÑARla A su CASA si NO quiEres QUE Te PASE ALgO MAlo

O sea, que la tarjeta no era falsa. Era verdadera. ¡Era una verdadera amenaza!

Todos los de la clase empezaron
a leerla con curiosidad y se la quitaban
de las manos unos a otros.

La profe terminó con el barullo
al entrar en el aula. Empezó
la clase, pero yo ya no
me acordaba de que era alumno.
Solo pensaba en que era detective
y habían amenazado a mi ayudante.

El caso de la tarjeta falsa
se estaba complicando.

Pensé que lo mejor era hacer una lista
de los enemigos de Ana y otra con los
enemigos de Pablo. Luego miraría
los que coincidían en las dos listas,
y entre ellos, seguro que encontraba
al malo, vamos, al culpable.

Mientras tanto hablaría con Irene.
«¿Qué tenía ella que ver con las
tarjetas?», pensaba yo, intrigado.

Irene me lo aclaró todo. Pablo y ella regresaban todos los días juntos porque viven en el mismo bloque. Eran amigos desde siempre y no tenía ni idea, pero ni idea, de a quién podía molestarle semejante cosa.

—A lo mejor –le dije yo– tienes un novio que está celoso.

—¿Novio celoso? Tú estás tarado. ¿No ves que soy muy pequeña para tener novio?

—Pues, entonces, un novio pequeño como tú.

—Pero ¡qué novio pequeño! No seas tonto. Lo que tienes que buscar es un loco de remate, y cuando lo encuentres, me lo dices, que quiero saber qué le pasa conmigo.

Y se fue.

Me dirigí entonces a Ana.
Ya había hecho su lista de enemigos.
La leí y, asombrado, exclamé:

—Ana, ¡qué barbaridad!
Pero cómo vas a tener...
¡diez enemigos! No puede ser.

Intenté convencerla de que lo pensara
mejor, que seguro que no tenía
tantos enemigos.

—Vamos a ver –me dijo–, un enemigo
es uno que te tiene manía o al que
tú le tienes manía y te quiere fastidiar,
¿sí o no?

Pues sí, eso es lo que yo entendía
por un enemigo.

—Bueno, pues estos son mis enemigos
–me dijo, y empezó a leer su lista
de nuevo.

Entonces se quedó pensativa
y tachó a Clara, a María, a Esteban,
a Yolanda, a Sergio, a Azucena...

«¡Bieeenn!», pensé yo.
Pero como Ana está un poco
como una cabra, añadió a Serguei,
a Alicia..., y le quité el papel cuando vi
que empezaba a escribir mi nombre.

—¡Pero cómo voy a ser tu enemigo
si soy tu detective!

—Es verdad –admitió–; además,
ya no me acuerdo de por qué eras
mi enemigo. Te quito, pero entonces
pongo a Pablo.

Pablo, mi ayudante, muy enfadado,
le gritó:

—Pero yo, ¿por qué?

Y Ana le recordó que le había aplastado
uno de sus lápices de cera.

—Fue sin querer, y además fue el curso pasado, y además soy ayudante de tu detective, y además ¡NO PUEDO SER SOSPECHOSO PORQUE YO TAMBIÉN HE RECIBIDO UNA TARJETA!, ¿vale?

Este argumento la convenció del todo.

Así que la lista de Ana quedó en seis compañeros de clase.

La lista de Pablo fue más difícil de elaborar. Se pasó toda una hora de clase pensando, y al final me vino con los nombres de dos personas. Ninguna coincidía con los enemigos de Ana, y para colmo me dijo:

—Bah, no te creas que son tan enemigos. Mejor los tacho.

Y los tachó.

Me miró y nos echamos a reír.
Así no podía empezar la investigación.

Entonces me propuso una idea
que me encantó. Colgaríamos un cartel
en la clase en el que pondríamos
que se buscaba a un sospechoso
de los gravísimos delitos de falsificación
y amenazas mediante el envío
de tarjetas.

Y lo firmaríamos los detectives:
Manu y Pablo.

Cuando los de la clase leyeran el cartel,
nos fijaríamos en sus caras, y el que se
pusiera colorado o estuviera nervioso,
¡ese sería el verdadero sospechoso!
Como en clase somos muchos,
vigilaríamos particularmente
a los de la lista de enemigos de Ana.

La investigación

O es fácil ser detective,
ni siquiera con ayudante.

Los de clase leyeron el cartel
y se entretuvieron haciendo
comentarios sobre los detectives
o sobre lo bonito que quedaba
lo de la mano negra, y entre ellos
empezaron a acusarse con bromas:

—Tú, eres tú.

—No, eres tú.

—Tú.

—No, tú.

O cosas así.

De manera que por más que
Pablo y yo nos fijamos en todos,
no pudimos sacar nada en claro.

Y eso no fue lo peor. Lo peor
fue que ese mismo día Serguei
(uno de los enemigos de Ana y,
por lo tanto, un sospechoso menos)
me entregó otra tarjeta.

¡Cómo no! ¡Estaba firmada
por la mano negra, el gorro rojo...!
Y lo que ponía era increíble.

Como las demás, estaba escrita con
letras recortadas de un periódico.
Y tenía un dibujo que, aunque muy mal
hecho, se entendía perfectamente:
un guante de boxeo enorme dándole
un puñetazo a la cara de un niño.

Una flecha con el nombre de Serguei
indicaba, por si había dudas, quién
era el que recibía el puñetazo.

Y junto al dibujo, una amenaza:

¿Qué estaba pasando? Serguei era
el mejor portero del mundo, o por
lo menos, era el mejor portero de
mi clase con muchísima diferencia...
¿Quién quería que se retirara?

Pablo y yo pensamos en los de la clase
de al lado, que siempre perdían
los partidos contra nosotros.
Entonces el malo tenía que ser alguien
del aula vecina.

Pero no. Tampoco podía ser porque
ese día les tocaba excursión.

Se habían ido de visita a una fábrica
de yogures. No había nadie,
y nadie podía haber dejado la tarjeta.

Pablo y yo nos quedamos en el recreo
mirando las tres tarjetas fijamente
y haciendo comentarios.

Mi padre me había dicho que los
detectives observan con mucha
atención y piensan sobre lo que ven.

—No son del mismo tamaño
–dijo Pablo.

—Una tiene un dibujo muy bonito;
otra, uno malísimo, y la otra no tiene
ni dibujo –dije yo.

Y así, una vez yo y otra Pablo,
estuvimos observando, pensando
y comentando:

—El color de la cartulina es distinto.

—La peor es la del puñetazo,
que asusta más.

—La tuya tiene una falta
de ortografía.

—¿La mano negra quiere decir
que no se lava?

—La del cumpleaños parece escrita
por una niña.

—¿Por qué?

—Es más cursi.

Y Ana, a la que habíamos dejado
sentarse junto a nosotros para que
viera cómo trabajan los detectives,
a condición de que estuviera callada,
pues no se calló y dijo:

—Tú sí que eres cursi y, además,
un machista.

Tuve que mirarla muy serio por encima
de mis gafas y pedirle silencio.

Mirar por encima de las gafas era
mi gesto favorito desde que me había
hecho detective.

Pero ya nos había desconcentrado y,
además, todas las observaciones
nos llevaban a la misma conclusión:
¡no teníamos ni idea de quién había
enviado esas tarjetas!

A todos los descartábamos como
sospechosos. Carlos no podía ser,
ya que era amigo de todos.

Marta, tampoco, porque nunca se
metía con nadie. Jimena, qué va, pues
qué le importaba a ella que Serguei
jugara o no al fútbol. Cecilia, ni hablar,
ya que su cumpleaños era en verano
y no lo celebraba... y así todos.
Por un motivo o por otro,
ninguno parecía sospechoso.

¿No sería la profe? La idea nos hizo
reír, pero nada más. También
la descartamos porque ella no
es capaz de hacer faltas de ortografía,
ni en broma.

Ana, aburrida y harta de estar callada,
preguntó:

—Y entonces, ¿quién puede ser?

«¡Y yo qué sé!».

Eso es lo que me entraron ganas de
contestarle, pero me acordé del casco
y me callé. Debía seguir la investigación.

Propuse escondernos en el armario
de clase antes de que subieran
los alumnos y pillar al malo
con las manos en la masa, es decir,
dejando una nueva tarjeta.

6

Despistados

AL día siguiente, el caso de las misteriosas tarjetas se complicó.

La profe nos echó una gran bronca por meternos en el armario y tirar las pinturas al suelo, aunque en realidad se habían caído sin querer y sin querer habían manchado el suelo de la clase. Pero, sin querer o queriendo, la bronca fue fenomenal.

Nadie dejó una tarjeta por la mañana, mientras espiábamos.

Fue peor. La dejó en la primera clase después de comer, cuando nosotros ya no espiábamos.

Pablo y yo estábamos desesperados,
desconcertados, desinformados,
desanimados, despistados...

Así lo escribimos en nuestra lista
del día, ya que como nos habíamos
acostumbrado a hacer listas
de sospechosos y no teníamos
ninguno, hicimos una lista
de cómo nos encontrábamos.

La última palabra que pusimos
fue *desnutridos*.

Nos dimos un poco de pena y nos
fuimos a la heladería a por un helado
de tres bolas para cada uno, pues
a Pablo le había dado dinero su abuela
por hacer dos recados. Dos recados,
seis bolas de helado, que estaban
buenísimas. Fue lo mejor del día.

Lo peor fue que la tarjeta nueva
nos dejó más despistados todavía,
si es que eso era posible.

Estaba dirigida a Delia. Y decía así:

> LA MANO NEGRA,
> EL GORRO ROJO,
> YO HAGO SIEMPRE
> LO QUE ES MI ANTOJO

Hasta ahí vale, pero ¡atención
a lo que seguía!:

> YO NO TENGO ANTOJO
> DE HACER LOS DEBERES
> TÚ ME LOS HARÁS
> TANTO SI QUIERES
> COMO SI NO QUIERES

La tarjeta iba acompañada de una hoja
de operaciones matemáticas,
que por lo visto Delia tenía que
resolver para el día siguiente
y dejar en la segunda papelera
del patio, nada más entrar,
a la derecha.

¡Qué caradura!
Estábamos indignados.

Y además, esto ponía la investigación
francamente difícil, porque
nos hacía sospechosos a todos
los de la clase.

Vamos, que a todos nos encantaría
que Delia nos hiciera los deberes.
Nunca se equivoca y tiene la letra
preciosa y dibuja bien y siempre
se sabe las preguntas. ¡Qué chollo!
Por un momento me entraron
ganas de ser yo la mano negra...

Me consolé, como siempre, pensando en mi casco. Además, Delia, con los ojos llorosos, me prometió que si encontrábamos al carota, nos invitaría al detective y a su ayudante a dos helados de tres bolas.

Era un buen aliciente para no abandonar el caso.

7

Espías

MANU, detective, o sea, yo,
y mi ayudante Pablo, también
detective, llegamos al colegio
con media hora de antelación.
Nos escondimos y vigilamos
la papelera del patio.

Vimos a Delia dejar en la papelera
la hoja de las cuentas matemáticas.
Nos había dicho que las iba
a resolver todas mal para que
se enterara la mano negra.

Vimos a un niño echar el envoltorio
de una chocolatina. Vimos al profe
de gimnasia dejar un periódico.

Vimos a una mamá tirar una piel
de plátano.

Y vimos a todos los compañeros
de clase alrededor de la papelera,
mirando fijamente sin ningún disimulo.

Todos sabían lo que pasaba
con la última tarjeta, pero como
no tienen ni idea de ser
detectives, nos estropearon
nuestra labor de espionaje.

Con toda la clase
vigilando, ¿cómo
se iba a descubrir
la mano negra
acercándose
a la papelera?

Salimos de nuestro escondite.
Y entonces Juan, al ver que
nos acercábamos a la papelera,
empezó a gritar:

—Ahí va, son ellos, ¡los detectives!
Se han hecho detectives para disimular.
¡Os hemos pillado!

Pablo se encargó de aclararle
las cosas, explicándole por qué
nosotros éramos los menos
sospechosos de todos. ¿Por qué?
Pues porque las cosas no son así,
los detectives nunca son los malos.
Son los que encuentran a los malos.

Y dicho esto, miró muy serio y
fijamente a cada uno de ellos,
poniendo cara de auténtico
investigador. Una mirada feroz
que creo que hizo que se dieran
la vuelta y se marcharan con aspecto
de sospechosos.

Mientras se alejaban, Pablo les gritó:

—Además, yo también he recibido una
tarjeta. ¿Cómo voy a ser el culpable?

Este argumento lo utilizaba tanto
que alguien podía pensar que sí,
que se había mandado la tarjeta
a sí mismo para disimular.

Alguien podía pensarlo, pero no yo.
Pablo era mi amigo y ayudante
de detective. De ninguna manera
lo pondría en la lista de sospechosos.

8

Morder el polvo

¡NI mi padre sabía resolver el caso de las tarjetas misteriosas!
Le pedimos ayuda, las miró,
las comparó y solo supo decir:

—¡Hay que ver cómo sois los niños
de ahora!

Pablo y yo nos miramos y protestamos
a la vez:

—¡Pero si nosotros no hemos sido!

—Ya, ya, pero ha sido alguien como
vosotros, de vuestra clase, ¿no?

—Sí.

—Pues eso, que vaya persona rara,
que invita a fiestas que no existen,
no quiere que Irene tenga amigos,
ni que el portero del equipo sea
bueno, ni quiere hacer los deberes...
Vamos, que no tengo ni idea
de qué le pasa a la mano negra esa.

Sí, lo cierto es que quien mandaba
las tarjetas era malo, malísimo,
y en mi clase, tan malo, malísimo,
la verdad es que no había nadie.
Todos tenemos nuestras cosas...
pero tan malos, tan malos...

Entonces Pablo dijo que lo más
seguro era que no fuera un niño,
porque somos más inocentes;
quizá sería un mayor, pues en todas
las películas se ve que entre
los mayores hay muchos más malos.

Así que hicimos una lista de
sospechosos entre los mayores

del colegio. Pusimos a todos
los profes que conocíamos,
a la conserje, a la secretaria,
a la directora y a la señora de la
limpieza. Y también al conductor
del autobús de la ruta, que siempre
está de mal genio, y si no es malo,
malísimo, por lo menos, lo parece.

Estábamos los detectives
discutiendo en el patio
sobre nuestra nueva lista.
La verdad es que no conseguíamos
imaginar que ninguno de nuestros
nuevos sospechosos tuviera
algún motivo
para escribir
esas tarjetas.
Y entonces ¡ocurrió!
A Pablo se
le había olvidado
el bocadillo
en la mochila
y subió a la clase
a por él.

Un minuto más tarde, asomado
por la ventana de la clase, me gritaba:

—¡Manu, corre, corre! ¡Ven rápido!

Vi claramente que algo grave sucedía
y subí como un rayo. Abrí la puerta
de la clase y ¡allí estaba! Una nueva
tarjeta sobre el primer pupitre.
Y sentado detrás, llorando, estaba
la mano negra, el gorro rojo.

—Le he pillado con las manos
en la mesa –dijo Pablo.

—En la masa, Pablo, se dice
«en la masa».

Y Pablo, que no, que era con
las manos en la mesa, en la mesa
de David, dejando una nueva tarjeta,
era como le había pillado.

Miré al sospechoso. Me dio como pena
y quise asegurarme de que era el
verdadero autor criminal de las tarjetas.

—¿Has sido tú, Carlos? –pregunté incrédulo, porque Carlos era uno de mis mejores amigos y muy bueno siempre con todos. ¿Cómo podía ser él la mano negra?

Y Carlos, muy disgustado, nos explicó lo que había pasado. Él había escrito sólo la última tarjeta, la que le estaba dejando a David, cuando le pilló Pablo. Lo decía de verdad: no tenía ni idea de las otras.

Y escuchamos con mucha atención toda su historia.

Resultaba que David tenía manía a Jorge, no se sabe por qué, y estaba todo el día molestándole. El día anterior le había llamado «gordo bombón» y se lo había escrito en su cuaderno de lengua, estropeándole la redacción que tenía que entregar. A Jorge se le habían saltado las lágrimas.

—Jorge es mi compañero
de pupitre –nos siguió explicando
Carlos– y me dio tanta pena,
que pensé que era una buena idea
aprovechar esto de las tarjetas
misteriosas. Así que la hice
ayer con letras de revista, como
las otras, y ahora se la estaba
dejando a David para que le
entrara miedo y dejara en paz a Jorge.
Pero me ha pillado Pablo.

En la tarjeta ponía: «David, o dejas
en paz para siempre, siempre, a Jorge
o morderás el polvo», y el dibujo que
incluía era un niño (supuestamente
David) tumbado en el suelo bocabajo,
y encima, una bota enorme que no
le dejaba levantarse.

Parece que «morder el polvo»
consiste en eso, en que te tiran
al suelo y te pegan una paliza.
A mí me pareció muy fuerte y miré
con ojos asombrados a Carlos.

—No lo iba a hacer. Era solo
para asustarle, hombre
–me aclaró Carlos.

Y la tarjeta, ¿quién la firmaba?
Pues sí, nada más y nada menos
que la mano negra, el gorro rojo.

—Pero Carlos, esta firma está mal
–dijo Pablo–. No pone lo de «yo hago
siempre lo que es mi antojo».

—¡Eso! «Yo hago siempre
lo que es mi antojo». ¡Claro!
–exclamó Carlos–. Si es que
no me acordaba de cómo era.
Estuve pensando en cosas
como «yo hago lo que quiero»,
«me porto como me da la gana»...
pero como no rimaban, lo dejé así.

—Pues esta no es auténtica –dije yo–;
es una tarjeta falsa.

Y los tres nos echamos a reír.

El caso es que Pablo y yo nos creímos
todo lo que nos había contado Carlos.
Es decir, que él sólo era el autor
de esa tarjeta y que de las anteriores
no sabía nada de nada.

Y entonces hicimos a Carlos
ayudante segundo de detective.
Porque se lo merecía.
Porque tuvo una idea genial.

9

Secreto profesional

ASÍ es como Carlos pasó de ser el malo, malísimo, a ser ayudante de detective y tener derecho a utilizar el casco que me había prometido Ana y a tomar helado de la invitación de Delia.
Fue cuando dijo:

—¡Claro, ya está! A lo mejor no hay un solo sospechoso. A lo mejor las otras tarjetas han sido escritas por distintas personas. Por ejemplo, la de Serguei la puede haber escrito Álvaro, que siempre se queda sin jugar porque el entrenador le dice que Serguei es mejor, y tampoco hay derecho a eso, ¿no?

No seguimos escuchándole.
Pablo y yo le dijimos que vale,
que podía ser detective él también,
y nos bajamos corriendo al patio
para buscar a Álvaro.

Cuando le encontramos,
le pedimos que nos acompañara.
Y allí, en la esquina del fondo del patio,
confesó.

Pero ¡hay que ver qué cosas
tenemos que hacer los detectives
para encontrar al culpable!

Le tuvimos que prometer a Álvaro
que, si nos decía la verdad, ¡le haríamos
a él también ayudante de detective!

A este paso, en mi clase iba a haber
más detectives que sospechosos,
pero bueno, tampoco me importaba.
Lo importante para un detective
es resolver el caso y, total, podíamos

repartir el uso del casco en diferentes días de la semana. Además, seis bolas de helado entre cuatro..., pues eso, a bola y media, que ya estaba bien.

Así que Álvaro admitió que era cierto. Que estaba harto, harto de que nunca le pusieran a él de portero, y que por eso le había dejado la tarjeta a Serguei, para ver si este año podía él jugar algún que otro partido.

Al detective primero, Manu, o sea, a mí, a su ayudante Pablo y a su segundo ayudante, Carlos, que también se había acercado a donde nos encontrábamos, nos dio pena. Pena o algo así.

Vamos, que nos parecía que tenía razón, que era injusto que siempre jugara el mismo. Así que le comprendimos. Le hicimos ayudante tercero, tal como le habíamos prometido, y le aseguramos que no se lo diríamos a nadie. Ni lo de Álvaro ni lo de Carlos, que para nosotros eso era secreto profesional.

Sí, se dice así, secreto profesional, que me lo dijo mi tía Pili, que tiene secreto profesional porque es periodista; y también tienen secreto profesional los médicos, los curas... y los detectives, que era lo que me interesaba a mí. Vamos, que te puedes callar, aunque te pregunte un mayor.

¿Está claro? Nadie iba a saber quién había escrito esas dos tarjetas.

10

Nuevas averiguaciones

¿Y el resto de las tarjetas? ¡Bah! El resto fue muy fácil.

Una vez que comprendimos que no era la misma persona la que quería que Serguei no fuera portero, que Irene no fuera amiga de Pablo, la que quería mandar una invitación de cumpleaños falsa a Ana, y además quería que le hicieran los deberes por la cara…, pues una vez entendido eso, fue todo facilísimo. Solo había que pensar y razonar.

¿Quién iba a querer que Delia le hiciera los deberes?

Bueno, toda la clase, vale. Pero
¿quién NECESITABA DE VERDAD
que Delia le hiciera los deberes
de matemáticas? Esa pregunta
nos hicimos los cuatro detectives
y los cuatro respondimos a la vez:

—¡Pedro!

Y es que hay que ver lo que le cuesta
a Pedro hacer bien las cuentas. Claro,
como es tan despistado, siempre se
le olvida si se lleva una o no, y no
se acuerda ni de la tabla de multiplicar.

En fin, que como las hace mal, la profe
le manda el doble que a los demás
y entonces les coge un asco
a las cuentas, que ya no puede más,
y en clase de matemáticas siempre
está muy agobiado.

Todo esto nos contó, y acabó
confesando que era el autor

de la tarjeta que obligaba
a Delia a hacer sus deberes.

Se le ocurrió esa idea cuando vio
lo de la mano negra... pero de las otras
tarjetas... ¡De las otras, él no tenía
ni idea!

Menos mal que todo esto Pedro
lo confesó sin tener que hacerle
detective. Solo nos pidió que por favor
no se lo dijéramos a nadie, que se
moría de vergüenza. Se lo prometimos.

Y también se lo prometimos a Diego.
Diego era el autor de la tarjeta que
había recibido Pablo.

Además, en el caso de Diego
¡lo había adivinado yo! Se trataba
de un novio celoso. Bueno, no era
novio de Irene, pero sí estaba celoso.
Vamos, que le gustaba Irene,
no sé por qué, y le daba envidia

que fuera tan amiga de Pablo,
tampoco sé por qué..., y que a él
casi ni le mirara. O eso le parecía
a él, que yo nunca me he fijado
si Irene me mira o no me mira.

A Diego, la verdad, no le entendíamos
muy bien, pero le dijimos que sí,
porque nos contaba todo esto
con la cara roja como un tomate,
que se veía que estaba pasando
vergüenza de verdad.

Y de verdad, le dijimos que no se
lo contaríamos ni a Irene ni a nadie.
Tampoco le dijimos a él quiénes
habían escrito las otras tarjetas.
Así que era lo justo.

Y ya estábamos como al principio.
¿Quién había mandado la tarjeta falsa
de cumpleaños?

Eso fue más difícil.
Pero cada vez éramos más listos
como detectives
y lo conseguimos.
Aunque nos costó
una larga
conversación
con Ana.

—Ana, ¿tú has enviado
a alguien alguna vez
una tarjeta falsa
de cumpleaños?

—Nooo. ¡A MÍ ME LA HAN ENVIADO!

—¿Alguien te ha pedido que
le invitaras a su cumpleaños
y tú no has querido?

—Al cumpleaños, cada uno invita
a quien quiere.

—Ya, Ana, ¿pero alguien te lo ha
pedido y has dicho que no?
Podría ser una venganza.

—No, porque yo digo muchas cosas
para que no parezca que soy tonta,
pero si alguien me lo pide, le invito
y ya está.

Y era verdad, que Ana es muy bocazas,
pero luego se arrepiente y es un trozo
de pan, como dice mi madre.

Y bueno, así estábamos dándole
vueltas, cuando parece que
a Ana se le encendió una luz
en el cerebro y dijo:

—Anda, pues la verdad es que un día
que María me hizo enfadar mucho,
no me acuerdo por qué, le dije que
era una mala persona, que no tenía
amigos, que nadie la quería y que por
eso nadie la invitaba a su cumpleaños.

¡Qué horror! La verdad es
que, visto así, bien se merecía
una tarjeta falsa, pero no se
lo dijimos y salimos corriendo
en busca de María.

Cuando nos vio llegar tan serios,
María dejó el grupo con
el que estaba jugando
y se acercó asustada a nosotros.

Le dije:

—María...

Y ya no tuve que decir nada más,
porque ella misma empezó a hablar:

—Sí, fui yo. Ya era hora de que lo
averiguarais; he estado todos estos
días muy preocupada. No podía más,
pensando a todas horas en la tarjeta
anónima. Estoy superarrepentida.

Ahora ya me habéis descubierto...
¡menos mal! Pero quiero que sepáis
que lo hice porque Ana me dijo cosas
muy feas y... pero, eh, ¡yo solo he
escrito una tarjeta, la del cumpleaños!
Del resto no tengo ni idea.

—Ya –le dijimos, y, como a los demás,
le prometimos que no se lo diríamos
a nadie.

Bueno, en este caso tendríamos
que decírselo a Ana, que nos había
contratado para investigar y que
además la perdonaría seguro.
Porque si no se lo decíamos, ¿cómo
íbamos a recibir el casco prometido?

Dejamos a María, pero yo me iba
inquieto porque estaba muy intrigado.
Así que me di la vuelta y le pregunté:

—María, ¿qué quiere decir eso de
«la mano negra, el gorro rojo, yo hago
siempre lo que es mi antojo»?

—«La mano negra» era para asustar
un poco; «el gorro rojo», porque
es mi color preferido, y lo otro...

Se quedó pensativa y confesó:

—Lo puse porque rimaba...
¡Me encanta la poesía!

—Así son las mujeres –dijo mi padre
cuando se lo conté.

O sea, que seguí sin entender nada.

11

Un caso resuelto

TAMBIÉN tuvimos que contarle
nuestro secreto a Delia,
para que nos invitara a los dos helados.
Pero en este caso solo le dijimos
que era alguien muy necesitado
el que le pedía que le hiciera
los deberes, alguien que prometía
no volver a hacerlo.

Y le pareció bien y no preguntó
nada más.

Yo creo que adivinó quién era porque
luego la vi explicarle un problema
de matemáticas a Pedro sin que
nadie se lo pidiera.

Informamos al resto de la clase de la resolución del caso en un gran cartel que escribimos. Lo hicimos poético, a propuesta de Carlos. Decía así:

El de las tarjetas falsas
es un caso ya resuelto.

No era uno, ni eran dos
los autores del enredo.

Que eran muchos
y por motivos diversos.

Escribir anónimos
es un asunto muy feo,
aunque todos tenían una razón
para hacer lo que hicieron.

«Nunca más habrá tarjetas»,
han dicho los que las escribieron,
porque resulta cobarde,
cobarde y un poco violento.

> Ahora piden perdón
> por hacer lo que hicieron.
> Así que todo queda resuelto.
>
> ¡Vivan los detectives
> Pablo, Álvaro, Manu y Carlos!,
> que con su gran ingenio
> investigar supieron
> y un caso muy difícil
> requetebién resolvieron.

Bueno, no rimaba mucho, pero no estaba mal. Nos costó muchísimo trabajo escribirlo porque es que la poesía es muy, muy difícil, casi tanto o más que ser detective, creo yo.

Los de la clase, al leer el cartel, empezaron otra vez a acusarse en broma:

—Has sido tú.

—No, tú.

—Tú.

—Tú has escrito la de Pablo.

—Y tú la de Ana...

Todos estaban en ese juego. Todos menos los detectives y los verdaderos autores de las tarjetas.

Ana se portó muy bien porque tampoco dijo nada, que me fijé, que desde que soy detective me fijo mucho en todo.

12

Seis bolas de helado y un casco

DECIDIMOS que era mejor que pusieran todas las bolas de helado en un mismo plato grande y nos dieran cuatro cucharillas, y así, todos juntos, con el plato en medio de la mesa, comimos un poco de cada bola, pues cada una era de un sabor.

El casco, que era precioso, nos
lo fuimos pasando y lo llevábamos
puesto un rato cada uno.

Estoy hablando de los cuatro
detectives, por la tarde del mismo
día en que informamos a la clase
de que el caso estaba resuelto.

Nos lo estábamos pasando
fenomenal. El casco, el helado,
el chocolate caliente por encima
que la heladera nos había regalado,
los amigos... y que no hubiera
en clase ningún malo, malísimo...,
todo me gustaba y
me daba risa.

Así que cuando se acercó Javier,
el del pupitre de atrás, a decirme:

—Manu, Manu, ¿sabes quién me
ha cogido mi súper cuaderno de
dibujo?

Simplemente le contesté:

—¡Y yo qué sé!

No estaba dispuesto a estropear ese momento maravilloso con la investigación de un nuevo caso.

Fin

alta mar

Taller de lectura

Manu, detective

1. Me encanta Manu

1.1. A mí, como a la autora del libro que tienes en tus manos… ¡me encanta Manu! ¿Y a ti? ¿Por qué?

....

1.2. Fíjate cómo describe la autora a Manu en la dedicatoria que ha escrito *Para ti:* «Es un niño normal, divertido, bueno, alegre… Pero no, no es solo eso; lo que más me gusta de Manu es que es ¡superpositivo! Siempre ve el lado bueno de las cosas; por eso, además de un buen detective, ¡está destinado a ser feliz! Y eso es muy contagioso».

Ahora te toca a ti. Describe a Manu.

....

....

1.3. En esta lista hay un montón de adjetivos. Selecciona los cinco que mejor caracterizan a Manu.

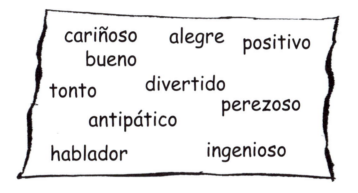

Y ahora, a ver si eres capaz de escribir los adjetivos que significan lo contrario de los que has seleccionado en la actividad anterior.

....

....

....

....

2. Dos buenos amigos de Manu

2.1. Pablo y Ana son dos buenos amigos de Manu. Y son muy distintos uno de otro. Explica las diferencias que se te ocurran entre la forma de ser de Pablo y la de Ana.

Pablo	Ana

2.2. ¿Crees que Pablo fue un buen ayudante de detective? ¿Por qué?

....

2.3. Opina sobre la reacción de Ana cuando recibe la tarjeta.

....

¿Cómo hubieras reaccionado tú?

....

3. Jugamos a detectives

Ahora vas a ser tú mi detective; vas a rastrear el libro capítulo a capítulo, página a página. ¡A ver cómo se te da!

3.1. Una tarjeta falsa

a) ¿Por qué Manu considera que la tarjeta que ha recibido Ana es falsa?

....

....

....

b) ¿Quién cree Ana que ha escrito la tarjeta falsa?

....

3.2. Primer sospechoso

a) ¿Qué opina Pablo de la tarjeta falsa cuando la ve?

....
....
....
....

b) ¿Qué tenía dibujada la tarjeta por delante?

....
....
....
....

c) ¿Qué pide Manu a Ana como pago por sus servicios de detective?

....
....

d) ¿Y qué le promete Ana?

....

3.3. Un verdadero caso de detective

a) Explica cómo es la familia de Manu.

....

....

b) ¿Crees que le toman en serio? ¿Crees que le apoyan con el asunto de las tarjetas falsas?

....

....

c) ¿Qué descubre Manu cuando cuenta lo de la tarjeta falsa en casa?

....

....

3.4. ¡Otra tarjeta!

a) ¿A quién le envían la segunda tarjeta?

....

b) Resume en tu cuaderno lo que ponía en ella.

c) ¿Crees que los niños tienen enemigos? ¿De verdad, de verdad lo crees? Haz una lista de tus enemigos y si te sale alguno explica por qué crees que es tu enemigo y pon al lado las cosas buenas que tiene. Quizá acabes por tacharlo de tu lista.

3.5. La investigación

a) Dibuja en tu cuaderno la tarjeta que recibe Serguei tal como tú te la imaginas.

b) ¿Qué tarjeta de todas las que se reciben tiene una falta de ortografía gordísima? Escribe la palabra correctamente.

....

....

....

c) ¿Por qué acusa Ana a Manu de machista? ¿Crees que tiene razón?

....

....

....

3.6. Despistados

a) Relee el capítulo 6. ¿Qué descubren Pablo y Manu desde el armario en el que se esconden?

....

....

....

b) Alguien ha estropeado la tarjeta que recibe Delia y no se lee bien. Completa las palabras que faltan para reconstruirla.

3.7. Espías

¿Crees que los compañeros de clase no hacen más que entorpecer la investigación? ¿Por qué? Comentadlo en clase.

3.8. Morder el polvo

a) Por fin avanza la investigación. ¿A quién descubre Pablo «con las manos en la mesa»?

....

b) ¿Por qué no usa Pablo la conocida expresión «con las manos en la masa»?

....

....

c) Las palabras *masa* y *mesa* se parecen mucho; solo cambia una letra. Así sucede con *caca* y *caco*, *cabra* y *cobra*, *musa* y *misa*. Añade tú nuevas parejas de palabras.

....

....

3.9. Secreto profesional

a) Pide a tu profesor o a tus padres que te expliquen qué es el secreto profesional.

b) Enumera, con la ayuda de tu profesor o de tus padres, profesiones en las que se está obligado a guardar el secreto profesional.

....

3.10. Nuevas averiguaciones

a) Ahora que ya ha acabado el intercambio de tarjetas haz un resumen de todas las que se reciben completando este cuadro:

Quién la recibe	Quién la ha escrito	Qué pretende conseguir
Ana		
Pablo		
Serguei		
Delia		
David		

b) Cada uno de los niños que escribe una tarjeta tiene un problema y busca una solución. Propón tú soluciones más adecuadas para cada caso.

- Ana: ....
  ....
- Pablo: ....
  ....
- Serguei: ....
  ....
- Delia: ....
  ....
- David: ....
  ....

c) Explica por qué no está justificado el envío de tarjetas, aunque con ellas los niños pretendieran conseguir cosas buenas.

....

....

3.11. Un caso resuelto

Nuestros detectives han preparado una poesía sobre la resolución del caso. Escribe tú nuevas rimas para informar a la clase de lo sucedido.

3.12. Seis bolas de helado y un casco

Y para acabar… prepara un posible encuentro con la autora de *Manu, detective.* Anota en tu cuaderno las preguntas que te gustaría hacerle.

Índice

La autora:
Pilar Lozano Carbayo   5
Dedicatoria *Para ti...*   7

Manu, detective
1. Una tarjeta falsa   9
2. Primer sospechoso   14
3. Un verdadero caso de detective   23
4. ¡Otra tarjeta!   30
5. La investigación   39
6. Despistados   48
7. Espías   54
8. Morder el polvo   59
9. Secreto profesional   68
10. Nuevas averiguaciones   73
11. Un caso resuelto   84
12. Seis bolas de helado y un casco   89

Taller de lectura   93

Series de la colección

Aventuras

Ciencia Ficción

Cuento

Humor

Misterio

Novela Histórica

Novela Realista

Poesía

Teatro

Títulos publicados

A partir de 8 años

- 7. Carlos MURCIANO. **La rana mundana** (Poesía)
- 29. Hilda PERERA. **Mumú** (Aventuras) •
- 30. Alfredo GÓMEZ CERDÁ. **Luisón** (Cuentos) •
- 37. Miguel Ángel MENDO. **Vacaciones en la cocina** (Cuentos) •
- 42. José Francisco VISO. **Don Caracol Detective** (Misterio) •
- 48. Lucila MATAIX. **El calcetín del revés** (Cuentos) •
- 59. Achim BRÖGER. **Mi 24 de diciembre** (Humor) •
- 66. Elvira MENÉNDEZ. **Ese no es mi zoo** (Humor) •
- 68. Braulio LLAMERO. **El rey Simplón** (Humor) •
- 77. Consuelo ARMIJO. **Guiñapo y Pelaplátanos** (Teatro)
- 85. Christine NÖSTLINGER. **Chachi** (Aventuras) •
- 112. Montserrat del AMO. **Mao Tiang** *Pelos Tiesos* (Cuentos) •
- 113. Pablo ZAPATA y Juan Luis URMENETA. **El cocodrilo Juanorro** (Aventuras)
- 118. Alfredo GÓMEZ CERDÁ. **Papá y mamá son invisibles** (Cuentos) •
- 119. Enric LLUCH. **Potosnáguel** (Aventuras) •
- 122. Manuel L. ALONSO. **Arturo ♥ Verónica** (Cuentos)
- 123. Concha BLANCO. **¡A mí qué me importa!** (Humor)
- 139. Manuel L. ALONSO. **Te regalo a mi hermano** (Aventuras) •
- 150. Concha LÓPEZ NARVÁEZ y Rafael SALMERÓN. **El príncipe perdido** (Aventuras) •
- 152. Alfredo GÓMEZ CERDÁ. **Tejemaneje y Estropajo** (Cuentos) •
- 156. Concha LÓPEZ NARVÁEZ. **Un puñado de miedos** (Cuentos) •
- 158. Alfredo GÓMEZ CERDÁ. **Soy… Jerónimo** (Cuentos)
- 159. Marinella TERZI. **Un año nada corriente** (Cuentos) •
- 165. Eliacer CANSINO. **El gigante que leyó El Quijote** (Cuentos) •

167. Concha LÓPEZ NARVÁEZ. **Ahora somos tres** (Cuentos) ●
169. Pilar LOZANO CARBAYO. **Manu, detective** (Misterio) ●
174. Pilar LOZANO CARBAYO. **Manu, detective, y el terror de Primaria** (Misterio) ●
180. Pilar LOZANO CARBAYO. **Manu, detective, y corazón piruleta** (Misterio)
182. Elvira MENÉNDEZ y José María ÁLVAREZ. **Una boa en El Paraíso** (Humor) ●
184. Concha BLANCO. **La vaca titiritera** (Cuentos)
189. Fernando LALANA y José A. VIDEGAÍN. **Chatarra imperial** (Humor) ●
195. Carmen VÁZQUEZ-VIGO. **El extraño caso del potingue rojo** (Misterio) ●
198. Pilar MOLINA LLORENTE. **A de Alas, A de Abuela** (Cuentos) ●
204. Carlos ELSEL. **El pichichi importado** (Humor) ●
208. Pilar LOZANO CARBAYO. **Manu, detective, en el zoo** (Misterio) ●
211. Concha LÓPEZ NARVÁEZ. **El último gol** (Aventuras)
218. José Francisco VISO. **Don Caracol Detective y el misterio del gallipato** (Misterio)
224. Fernando LALANA. **El genio de la botella de gaseosa** (Humor) ●
227. Dan GUTMAN. **La señorita Riqui es un poco friqui** (Humor) ●
230. Joaquín LONDÁIZ MONTIEL. **El Caballero de las Letras** (Aventuras)
233. J. R. BARAT. **Luna de mazapán** (Poesía)
237. Eliacer CANSINO. **El maravilloso señor Plot** (Aventuras) ●

● Dispone de cuaderno de Lectura Eficaz.

También te gustarán

Otros libros de la Serie Manu, detective

Manu, detective, y el terror de Primaria.
Pilar Lozano Carbayo. Colección Altamar, n.º 174

Este curso promete ser muy pero que muy divertido... Hasta que irrumpe en la clase un desconocido: un señor alto, delgado, moreno y con unos ojos superpenetrantes... que resulta ser nada más y nada menos que ¡el nuevo profe! Con él las cosas ya no van a ser igual, sobre todo cuando se produce en el cole una extraña desaparición... Manu, detective, y su ayudante Pablo se dedican a investigar. ¿Serán capaces de resolver este nuevo caso? Recorre las divertidas páginas del libro y lo descubrirás.

Otros libros de la Serie Manu, detective

Manu, detective, y corazón piruleta.
Pilar Lozano Carbayo. Colección Altamar, n.º 180

Manu y los de su clase hacen una excursión muy emocionante... ¡a una fábrica de caramelos! Está a rebosar de golosinas de todos los colores: regalices, gominolas, chicles... y, lo mejor de todo, ¡piruletas corazón! Pero lo que parecía un día inolvidable acaba convirtiéndose en un lío tremendo para Manu, pues deberá descubrir al culpable de un extrañísimo robo. ¿Serán Manu y su ayudante Pablo capaces de resolver este nuevo caso? Abre el libro, recorre sus páginas y verás qué magnífica tarde de misterios y de risas pasas con ellos.

Alaska's KENAI PENINSULA

A TRAVELER'S GUIDE

Text by Andromeda Romano-Lax
Photos by Greg Daniels & Bill Sherwonit

ALASKA NORTHWEST BOOKS™

*To Christine, Jeff, Karen, and Stewart:
co-adventurers, and gracious providers
of post-Peninsula meals and beds.*

ACKNOWLEDGMENTS—Thanks to B.L., A.L. and T.L, for companionship; Greg Daniels and Bill Sherwonit for their excellent photography; Marybeth Holleman for early idea-sharing; Mina Jacobs and the staff of the Anchorage Museum of History and Art for help finding historical photos; Ellen Wheat, Don Graydon, and Tricia Brown for editorial guidance; and, for sharing information on wildlife and land management, the Alaska Public Lands Information Center, Alaska Department of Fish and Game, John Schoen at the Alaska office of the National Audubon Society, and Heather Johnson-Schultz at the U.S. Fish and Wildlife Service.
—A.R.L.

Text © 2001 Andromeda Romano-Lax
Photographs © 2001 Greg Daniels, © 2001 Bill Sherwonit, and others, as credited
Book compilation © 2001 by Alaska Northwest Books™
An imprint of Graphic Arts Center Publishing Company
P.O. Box 10306, Portland, Oregon 97296-0306, 503-226-2402
www.gacpc.com

All rights reserved. No part of this book may be reproduced or transmitted in any form or by any means, electronic or mechanical, including photocopying, recording, or by any information storage and retrieval system, without written permission of the publisher.

The name Alaska Northwest Books and the caribou logo are trademarks of Graphic Arts Center Publishing Company.

Library of Congress Cataloging-in-Publication Data
Romano-Lax, Andromeda, 1971–
    Alaska's Kenai Peninsula / Andromeda Romano-Lax, Bill Sherwonit, Greg Daniels.
        p. cm. — (Alaska pocket guide)
Includes bibliographical references and index.
    ISBN 0-88240-527-6
    1. Kenai Peninsula (Alaska)—Guidebooks. I. Sherwonit, Bill, 1950–
II. Daniels, Greg, 1943–   III. Title. IV. Series.
    F912.K4 R65 2001
    917.98'3—dc21

2001000174

PHOTOS—*Front cover:* Fly-fishing calm waters (© Greg Daniels); *Endpages:* A Cook Inlet sunset, with Redoubt volcano (© Greg Daniels); *Page 3:* Kenai moose browse in a frosty pond (© Greg Daniels); *Page 5:* Hands full of salmonberries (© Andromeda Romano-Lax); *Back cover:* The author paddles with Augustine volcano in the background (© Brian Lax).

President/Publisher: Charles M. Hopkins
Editorial Staff: Douglas A. Pfeiffer, Ellen Harkins Wheat, Timothy W. Frew, Tricia Brown, Jean Andrews, Kathy Matthews, Jean Bond-Slaughter
Production Staff: Richard L. Owsiany, Susan Dupere
Designer: Constance Bollen, cb graphics
Map: Gray Mouse Graphics

Printed in Hong Kong

Contents

THE KENAI PENINSULA: A MICROCOSM OF ALASKA / 7

Map / 10

KENAI PENINSULA AT A GLANCE / 13

KENAI GEOGRAPHY:
RIVERS RUN THROUGH IT, WATERS SURROUND IT / 21

FIRST SALMON, FIRST PEOPLES / 33

KENAI HISTORY: FUR, GOLD, AND OIL / 41

FLORA: SHAPED BY FIRE AND ICE / 55

WILDLIFE OF LAND AND STREAM / 63

WILDLIFE OF SEA AND SKY / 73

THE COMMUNITIES OF TODAY:
WORK HARD, PLAY HARD / 85

Recommended Reading / 92

Index / 93

The Kenai Peninsula: A Microcosm of Alaska

In Anchorage, we lean south toward the Kenai Peninsula for good reason. In darkest winter, that's where the low-arcing sun hides, a dim orb taunting us from afar. But beginning each spring—aah, spring—that's the direction we turn to find so many other wonderful things as well: fish and berries, trails and wildlife, a thousand secret places to walk or paddle or listen to the music of glacier-fed creeks splashing across rounded stones.

Every May in the forest understory, a dozen shades of green spread and rise like the tide itself. The growing season is short, and the plants know it. We know it, too, and we can't bear to waste time. By summer, we're migrating to the campgrounds, rivers, beaches, and trails of the Kenai in droves, as explorers, prospectors, and anglers have been doing for two and a half centuries. The first European seekers came looking for a Northwest Passage. It's not here, of course, as the 18th-century explorer Captain Cook realized after he wearily decided to "turn again" at the head of what we now call Turnagain Arm. Later the Peninsula tantalized newcomers with promises of gold, trophy-sized fish, and solitude—rewards you can still find.

Exit Glacier pours through a tundra-covered valley in Kenai Fjords National Park.

◀ © Bill Sherwonit

The Kenai's easy access makes it an obvious destination for Alaska residents and visitors alike. Ironically, though, easy access obscures just as many of the Peninsula's finest attractions. Smooth highways and roadside espresso stands make it tempting to speed south until you find a crowded roadside spot where the fish are biting, or until you reach asphalt's end in the seaside towns of Seward and Homer. But by rushing, you miss out on the Kenai's secret: The Peninsula is a microcosm of Alaska. Somewhere within its far-ranging boundaries you can get a taste of nearly every landscape and wildlife wonder our state has to offer. Not just fish and forest, but fjords, calving glaciers, ice fields, and alpine tundra. Not just moose, but caribou, beluga whales, sea otters, seabirds, eagles, and far more.

On the Peninsula, you can discover Alaska's past, as a wilderness first prized for its extractable resources, later appreciated as refuge for both animals and humans. You can meet its diverse people, including the descendants of Athabascan, Alutiiq, Russian, and American settlers.

You can find crowds on the Kenai Peninsula . . .

. . . and you can find solitude.

On the Peninsula, you can see Alaska's future, too. The Kenai offers a look at how people and wilderness can exist side by side. Just a couple of hours' drive from the heart of Peninsula is Anchorage, with a population of more than 260,000 residents, and twice that many tourists visit the Peninsula each summer. Yet fish, moose, and brown bears thrive here. Anglers and hunters have recognized the Kenai as a wilderness worth protecting for nearly a century. Conservation programs help maintain a balance that serves both wildlife and human needs.

The Kenai's parklands, refuges and wild spaces are so vast that you could slip Vermont into the Kenai's interior and overlap only one major road. The southern Kenai coast, most of it sculpted by glaciers and unreachable by road, offers even more ways to experience the real Alaska away from the crowds. What is true of our state as a whole is true of the Kenai in particular: The farther you are willing to go, the more you will find. Stick to the highways, and you will see a remarkable sampling of Alaska landscapes. Head off the main roads, and you will take part in the exploratory spirit that is synonymous with this frontier state. ■

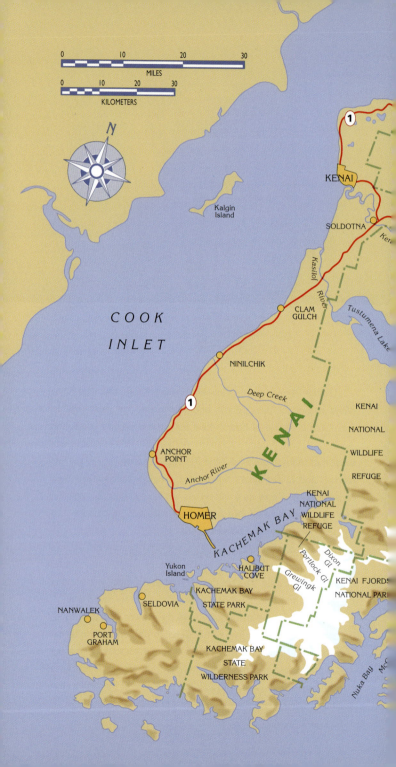

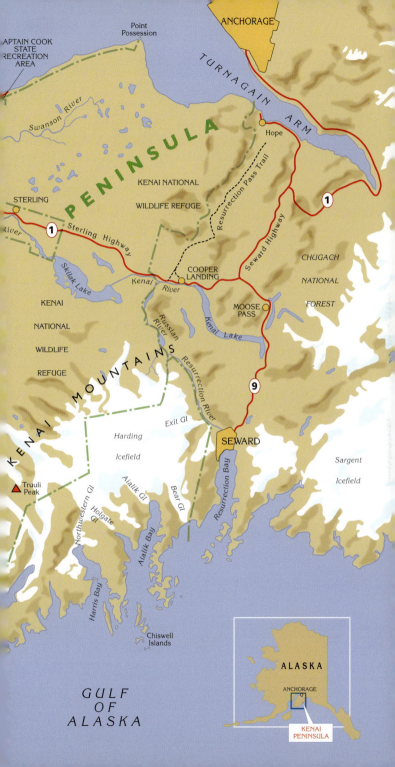

Kenai Peninsula at a Glance

Size: 9,000 square miles.

High point: 6,612 feet, at the summit of Truuli Peak on the northwestern edge of Harding Ice Field.

Climate: Summers are cooler and winters are warmer than in Interior Alaska. Summer daytime temperatures range from the high 40s to the low 70s Fahrenheit—coolest along the southern coast, warmer inland. In winter, daytime temperatures range from 30 below zero to 30 above. The Kenai's mountainous eastern half is wetter than the western half. While Seward in the east averages 67 inches of precipitation a year, the west-side town of Homer gets 25 inches and the town of Kenai sees only 19. Wherever you go, a warm hat, fleece jacket, waterproof shell, and waterproof boots will make your stay more comfortable.

Hours of daylight: 19 maximum in summer, 5 minimum in winter.

Location and access: The Kenai Peninsula is located in Southcentral Alaska, about 50 miles south of Anchorage. It is accessible by car along the Seward Highway, as well as by bus and train from Anchorage. Regularly scheduled air service is available from Anchorage to Kenai-Soldotna, Seward, and Homer.

A Seward-based tour boat brings visitors to the Holgate Glacier.

The Alaska Railroad offers scenic summer rail service between Anchorage and Seward along a 114-mile route that climbs mountain passes and skirts several glaciers.

Driving notes: Two major highways bisect the Kenai Peninsula. The 127-mile-long Seward Highway, one of Alaska's most scenic routes, connects Anchorage with Seward. Ninety miles south of Anchorage, the Sterling Highway branches off from the Seward Highway and continues for 143 miles to Homer. Both highways are open year-round, though avalanches can close the Seward Highway for short periods. On the Seward Highway, motorists are required to drive with headlights on at all times. On both highways, backups caused by slow vehicles are common. To look for roadside wildlife, take the detour off the Sterling Highway and onto Skilak Lake Loop Road, where hunting is restricted and animals are frequently spotted. Also, look for signed pull-outs along both highways.

Visitor centers: The Begich, Boggs Visitor Center in Portage, en route to the Kenai Peninsula from Anchorage, is the state's most-visited attraction, offering views of Portage Glacier, observation decks with spotting scopes, interpretive trails, and exhibits on glaciers and wildlife. The Kenai Fjords National Park Visitor Center at Seward's small boat harbor has a good bookshop and people who can answer your questions about the park. The Kenai National Wildlife Refuge Visitor Center in Soldotna offers maps and wildlife-watching brochures that will help you find the less-traveled trails of the refuge. Soldotna also has its own Visitor Information Center, in the center of town on the Sterling Highway. The Kenai Visitors and Cultural Center in the town of Kenai offers art exhibits and information on bed-and-breakfasts, fishing charters, and other local attractions. On the highway leading into Homer you'll find the Alaska Maritime National Wildlife Refuge Visitor Center, with displays, a small theater, and summer programs.

Bird-watching: In early May, hundreds of thousands of migrating shorebirds descend on Kachemak Bay, near Homer. The best time to spot seabirds is June through August, and boat tours are available to viewing sites including the Chiswell Islands, near Seward, and Kachemak Bay. Good roadside bird-watching spots

PARKLAND MOSAIC

STUDY A MAP OF THE KENAI PENINSULA and you'll see a confusing array of dashed and dotted lines—the boundaries of state and federal lands. Most of the Peninsula is undeveloped public property. Towns are few and far between. On the map they appear as mere pinpricks, tiny gateways to a large and bountiful backcountry that is open to all.

Chugach National Forest dominates the Peninsula's eastern half, reaching across neighboring Prince William Sound all the way to Cordova. At 6 million acres, the Chugach is second in size only to Southeast Alaska's Tongass National Forest among the national forests of the United States.

The 2-million-acre Kenai National Wildlife Refuge forms most of the north and central parts of the Kenai, including the lands surrounding Tustumena Lake. The refuge's southeast boundary is a jagged line formed by the Kenai Mountains.

From these mountains southeast to the Gulf of Alaska is Kenai Fjords National Park, a mostly ice-dominated wilderness that includes 10 glaciers in its 570,000 acres.

Kachemak Bay State Park and Kachemak Bay State Wilderness Park constitute a slice of the Kenai's southernmost lobe of land, extending from the south shore of Kachemak Bay to the Gulf of Alaska.

Kachemak Bay State Park is accessible by boat or plane only. But most of the Kenai's public lands are bisected by scenic highways. The Sterling Highway—which ends at Homer, on Kachemak Bay—slices through Kenai National Wildlife Refuge, offering the motorist glimpses of lake-dotted woodlands.

In 2000, the Seward Highway was named an All-American Road—a top honor among our nation's most beautiful roads. No other Alaska highway has won such recognition. Traveling the Seward Highway's 127-mile length, you drive through Chugach National Forest and up to the glacier-bound edge of Kenai Fjords National Park.

Along both the Seward Highway and the Sterling Highway are dozens of scenic pullouts, interpretive displays, and trailheads, beckoning you to get a more intimate view of the Kenai's prodigious parklands. ■

Rafters ride the rapids on Sixmile Creek.

include Tern Lake at the junction of the Seward and Sterling Highways, Skilak Lake Loop Road near Cooper Landing, Warren Ames Bridge in Kenai, Anchor River Road in Anchor Point, and the Homer Spit. More than 200 bird species have been tallied in the Chugach National Forest.

Fishing: An Alaska fishing license, purchased easily from most grocery stores, gas stations, and sporting goods shops, is required for all fishing. An additional king salmon fishing tag is required to pursue Alaska's largest salmon species. Fishing opportunities include river angling for salmon and rainbow trout, especially on the Kenai and Russian Rivers. Lakes in the Chugach National Forest and Kenai National Wildlife Refuge offer more secluded fishing for grayling, arctic char, lake trout, and rainbow trout. Deep-sea halibut charters depart from several Cook Inlet and Kachemak Bay communities. The Seward Silver Salmon Derby (August) and the Homer Jackpot Halibut Derby (May 1 to Labor Day) offer cash prizes to ticket holders who catch the largest fish. Contact the

Alaska Department of Fish and Game at (907) 267-2898 for fishing updates and regulations.

Hunting: Licensed hunting is allowed on some Kenai Peninsula public lands. Species include caribou, moose, black bear, Dall sheep, mountain goat, and ptarmigan. Contact the Alaska Department of Fish and Game at (907) 267-2898 for regulations.

Paddling: The 60-mile Swan Lake Route and the 80-mile Swanson River Route are both part of the popular Kenai National Wildlife Refuge Canoe Trail System, allowing canoeists and kayakers to get away from the crowds and spot more reclusive loons, bears, moose, and, rarely, wolves. Sea kayakers can explore miles of coastline along Resurrection Bay and the south shore of Kachemak Bay, or can arrange remote drop-offs in Kenai Fjords National Park. Canoe and kayak rentals and guided sea kayaking tours are available throughout the Kenai Peninsula. Cooper Landing and Hope are the respective starting points for guided raft and kayak trips on the Kenai River (Class I-III) and Sixmile Creek (Class III-V).

Hiking and mountaineering: The Kenai Peninsula has over 300 miles of developed hiking trails and many more backcountry paths. The 38-mile Resurrection Pass Trail is the Peninsula's most popular multi-day hike through the Chugach National Forest. Linked with the Russian Lakes and Resurrection River Trails, it is a 7- to 10-day trek from Hope to Exit Glacier near Seward. The 23-mile Johnson Pass Trail is another popular overnight hike in the Kenai Mountains. The 15-mile combined Primrose and Lost Lake Trails, near Seward, offer good views of the alpine countryside. Kachemak Bay State Park, the Kenai National Wildlife Refuge, and the Caines Head State Recreation Area near Seward have networks of trails. Kenai Fjords National Park, best visited by boat, has few developed trails, with the exception of the half-mile path to the face of Exit Glacier and a steep and snowy 5-mile (one-way) trail to the Harding Ice Field, at 3,500 feet. From trail's end, well-equipped mountaineers can venture farther onto the ice field.

Camping: The U.S Forest Service maintains backcountry campsites and more than a dozen roadside campgrounds near Hope and along the Seward and Sterling Highways. Campgrounds closest to the Kenai and Russian Rivers fill early. Slightly less crowded are the Kenai National Wildlife Refuge campgrounds on the Skilak Lake Loop Road. The National Park Service operates a tents-only campground on the road to Exit Glacier. Kachemak Bay State Park has rustic tent sites. Seward, Homer, Kenai, Soldotna, Anchor Point, Ninilchik, Clam Gulch, Kasilof, and the Captain Cook State Recreation Area have waterfront campgrounds and/or rustic campsites that tend to be mobbed during salmon runs, and quiet the rest of the summer. For more information, contact land agencies directly or visit the Alaska Public Lands Information Center in downtown Anchorage, 405 W. 4th Ave., Suite 105; or call (907) 271-2737.

Public cabins: Backcountry travelers who prefer a rustic roof to a tent should consider reserving a no-frills public cabin. Visit the Alaska Public Lands Information Center in Anchorage or call the following numbers: for Forest Service cabins, (877) 444-6777; for State Park cabins, (907) 269-8400; for Kenai Fjords National Park cabins, (907) 224-3175.

Boat tours: Large cruise ships dock in Seward. Smaller sightseeing boats depart daily in summer from Seward for half-day and daylong tours of Resurrection Bay and the Kenai Fjords. Sightseeing boats as well as water taxis depart Homer daily in summer for trips across Kachemak Bay.

Scenic flights: Flights over the Harding Ice Field originate in Seward. From Homer, flights are offered to Seldovia and the glacier country of Kachemak Bay State Park. Flight operators in Homer also offer bear-viewing trips across Cook Inlet to the Alaska Peninsula.

Other activities: Horseback riding on Homer Spit and western Kenai beaches; cross-country skiing and snow-machining in the north and central Peninsula; year-round guided dog mushing in the Seward area; mountain biking on Chugach National Forest trails. ■

Kenai Peninsula at a Glance

Driving the Sterling Highway in autumn.

Kenai Geography: Rivers Run Through It, Waters Surround It

The Kenai has so many faces that I have difficulty pinpointing its essence. Then, on a late fall day, I sift through my summer vacation photos and am struck by a single fact: Water glistens in every picture. A rowboat placidly floats on platinum waters near Seldovia. Harlequin ducks paddle-kick past roiling jade-colored eddies as they cross the Kenai River. From a mountain-rimmed overlook in the central Kenai, glacial lakes reflect the deep blue of a brilliant summer sky.

But why should I need photographs to remember? At summer's end, Cook Inlet sand still clings to the creases of my hip waders; the deep hatches of my sea kayak still bear the tangy scent of Kachemak Bay saltwater. You may catch a lingering whiff of fish from my car's trunk. The Kenai Peninsula wouldn't be Alaska's favorite place for recreation without its seacoast, lakes, and streams.

If not for the 10-mile-wide isthmus connecting Portage to Whittier—and separating Turnagain Arm from Prince William Sound—the Kenai Peninsula would be an island. Turnagain Arm forms the Peninsula's northern boundary, a liquid margin that

A tide pool captures a Kenai Peninsula sunset.

changes dramatically with the tides. Cook Inlet, a 220-mile-long estuary, laps against the Peninsula's mostly straight western boundary, a coast of clamming beaches and coal-seamed bluffs. To the south and east, away from most roads, glaciers have clawed the coast into isolated, steep-walled fjords, now submerged and flooded by the sea.

A fly fisherman casts for rainbow trout on the Kenai River.

THE WATERS OF COOK INLET

COOK INLET AND ITS BAYS are shallow but broad, covering about 10,000 square miles—roughly the size of the state of Virginia. Within this silt-laden, watery realm lives a complex web of life, fed by extreme tides and complicated currents. Salmon, as well as pollution, travel along major tidal rips. Upwelling near islands at the mouth of Cook Inlet draws nutrients from the deeper Gulf of Alaska. These upwelled waters create circular surface currents in Kachemak Bay, making it a place of exceptionally high marine productivity. This bay off the southwest Kenai Peninsula coast, by Homer, has been designated a National Estuarine Research Reserve and a Western Hemisphere Shorebird Reserve. ■

Water surrounds the Kenai and flows through it as well. The Peninsula is a commonwealth of lakes and streams, some of them glittering with traces of gold, and many more brimming with fish. Stateliest of all is the Kenai River itself, an 83-mile-long artery that links the Peninsula's mountainous eastern flanks with the flatlands of the west. The river begins near the roadside community of Cooper Landing, where it drains boomerang-shaped Kenai Lake. From the start, its waters are an unearthly, opaque blue-green, made milky by the fine silt delivered from the river's glacial headwaters.

For a dozen miles, the Kenai River runs parallel to the Sterling Highway, offering throngs of fishermen easy access to runs of sockeye salmon. The densest angling action occurs midway down this accessible stretch, at the confluence with the Russian River, a clearwater tributary. A half-dozen miles past the Russian River, the Kenai River takes an unexpected twist, shooting through a canyon and spilling into another large body of water, Skilak Lake.

Fifteen-mile-long Skilak Lake is also blue-green and glacier-cold. Like Kenai Lake, Skilak Lake is a key nursery area and winter sanctuary for salmon. The Lower Kenai River, west of Skilak Lake, winds through the neighboring cities of Soldotna and Kenai, where

Anglers flock to the Kenai River for the challenge of king fishing.

homes and businesses crowd its fragile shores, before emptying into Cook Inlet. At its lower reaches, the river vibrates with the traffic of drift boats. Anglers cruise the lower river and cast from its banks for king salmon, the Kenai's largest and most prized species. A 97-pound king salmon was hoisted out of these picturesque waters in 1985.

The Kenai and Russian Rivers are world-famous. Just to the north and south are hundreds of other streams, ponds, and glacial lakes that are famously obscure. The Peninsula's northwest corner appears on maps like a sponge. Canoeists, moose, and natural gas drilling sites share this less-visited, lake-dotted area, a landscape flattened and pockmarked by receding glaciers of long ago. South of the Kenai River, 22-mile-long Tustumena Lake lies within the Kenai National Wildlife Refuge. No roads crowd its shores. Most visitors fly in or boat in from a launch near the lake's western outlet.

The only sizable areas of the Kenai without flowing water are locked in ice. More than a tenth of the Peninsula is glaciated. The Harding Icefield is a 700-square-mile white cap dominating the Kenai Mountains near Seward, pierced only by the exposed tops of the glacier-surrounded mountains known as *nunataks* ("lonely peaks"). This ice field feeds glaciers that flow into arms of the

ACROSS THE ICEFIELD

THOUGH NATIVE ALASKANS used several Kenai Peninsula glaciers as transportation routes—most notably Portage Glacier connecting Prince William Sound and Turnagain Arm—the Harding Icefield deterred modern explorers. That began to change in 1936 when Yule Kilcher arrived in Seward.

The mile-high ice field was one of the first spectacles that caught his attention, but he had more serious matters in mind. Too antsy to wait for the coastal steamer to Homer, where he planned to settle, the Swiss immigrant made the trip on foot instead, staying clear of glaciers as he walked north, then west, and then south to Kachemak Bay. He claimed land near Homer, and then returned to Seward just months later. At that time, Kilcher spent a week unsuccessfully attempting to cross the ice field before returning home.

He didn't forget the Harding, though. More than three decades later, in 1968, Kilcher tried again. He set out with a party of nine others. Six turned back, but Kilcher and three companions—Bill Babcock, Dave Johnston, and Vin Hoeman—hiked all the way from Chernof Glacier east to Exit Glacier, traversing the immense ice field. Along the way, the party also made a first ascent of Truuli Peak, at 6,612 feet the Kenai Peninsula's highest point.

Kilcher's other claim to fame: He's the grandfather of pop singer Jewel.

Female harlequin ducks dodge riffles in the Kenai River.

Gulf of Alaska. The Harding is a huge remnant of the ice ages, when glaciers advanced over the Kenai Peninsula and melted back at least 7 times.

The signs of repeated glacial scouring can be seen at various sites around the Peninsula. Rolling mounds visible from the Seward Highway south of Turnagain Pass are glacial moraines—ridges of silt, sand, and gravel left by receding glaciers. Three successive moraines are visible along the Sterling Highway near Soldotna. Large boulders deposited by receding glaciers—called glacial erratics—dot the tidal flats in Captain Cook State Park.

The Sargent Icefield supplies glaciers spilling into Prince William Sound, east of the Kenai Peninsula. The Grewingk-Yalik Icefield, a shiny meringue of snow and ice, is visible across Kachemak Bay, tantalizing adventurers camped on the Homer Spit. Even in summer, when fly fishers strip to T-shirts and hikers scramble through lush forest foliage, the cold face of winter stares down from high peaks. Standing hip-deep in the rushing Kenai River or watching white slabs tumble off tidewater glaciers in Kenai Fjords National Park, visitors observe firsthand the movement of water and ice, powerful shapers of this northern landscape.

Other forces have shaped the Kenai Peninsula as well. Alaska is part of the Ring of Fire, a band of seismic and volcanic activity arcing around the Pacific Basin. From various roadside pull-offs along the Peninsula's western shore you can gaze across Cook Inlet and see four of Alaska's volcanoes: Redoubt, Iliamna, Spurr, and Augustine. Although these smoldering, snow-covered giants do not stand on the Peninsula itself, they form the most recognizable part of the Peninsula skyline, and they live squarely in every resident's consciousness. That's because the geologically young volcanoes have spewed mushroom clouds of ash, rock, and gas on several occasions, blanketing towns in debris.

Redoubt Volcano, the 10,197-foot peak visible from the town of Kenai, erupted most recently from late 1989 through April 1990. Ash covered parts of the Kenai Peninsula and the Matanuska-Susitna Valley north of Anchorage, and oil production was curtailed on 10 platforms in Cook Inlet.

Morning reflection on Crescent Lake.

ALASKA'S KENAI PENINSULA

"Ghost trees" frame the head of a Nuka Bay lagoon.

THE BIGGEST EARTHQUAKE

ONE OF ALASKA'S WORST natural disasters started when residents expected it least: on a quiet spring evening, just two days before Easter. At 5:36 P.M. on March 27, 1964, the streets of Seward began to shake gently. In seconds, the jarring motion intensified and the ground began to undulate. Streets buckled and buildings swayed. Avalanches roared down the steep canyons overlooking Resurrection Bay. Along the waterfront, offshore landslides and seismic sea waves (tsunamis) unleashed even greater destruction. Fishing boats were thrown hundreds of feet inland. Shorefront storage tanks ruptured and fire roared through the muddy wreckage.

Twelve people were killed in Seward by the effects of this earthquake—with a magnitude of 9.2, the most powerful ever recorded in North America. Seward was the only Kenai Peninsula town to suffer fatalities, but elsewhere in Alaska, 103 people died. Tsunamis claimed 16 more lives in California and Oregon. Some parts of the coast were thrust up, while other shorelines, including the Seward waterfront, dropped from 3 to 6 feet.

The earthquake struck on the day known as Good Friday—and coincidentally, the *Exxon Valdez* oil spill also occurred on Good Friday, 25 years later, and not far from the earthquake's epicenter, in northern Prince William Sound. The timing of the earthquake can be considered fortunate. When the shaking and flooding struck, schools were closed, most business areas were uncrowded, and the tide was low. If not for these factors, in addition to the sparsity of Southcentral Alaska's population, the death toll might have been far greater.

Alaskans rebuilt their towns with speed and determination. In fact, Seward's modern-day vigor seems an outgrowth of its zeal to rebuild and reclaim its status as a small but critical transportation hub. But signs of the big quake are still visible on the Kenai Peninsula. Notice the "ghost trees" near Portage, along the Seward Highway at the head of the Peninsula. These and other pockets of dead, sun-bleached coastal timber show where the land dropped, inundating tree roots with deadly saltwater. ■

ALASKA'S KENAI PENINSULA

Mount Redoubt is silhouetted against a Cook Inlet sunset.

Augustine Volcano, which occupies its own uninhabited island in Kamishak Bay, has been Cook Inlet's most active volcano. Visible from Homer, this 4,025-foot-high volcano has erupted seven times since 1812, most recently in 1986. The 1883 eruption created a 30-foot-high tsunami that struck Nanwalek—fortunately at low tide. The wall of water claimed no lives, but coastal residents are apprehensive about future waves that could be unleashed by Augustine. Mount Iliamna, its 10,016-foot neighbor, hasn't erupted in modern times.

Due west of Anchorage, Mount Spurr is nonetheless close enough to threaten the Kenai Peninsula with ash. The 11,100-foot volcano kept residents guessing between June and September of 1992, when it erupted repeatedly after 39 years of inactivity. Ashfall delayed air traffic, but otherwise, damages were minimal compared to the 1989-90 Redoubt blasts, which cost the nation $100 million.

In the distant past, a lesser-known volcano exploded even more violently. About 3,600 years ago, the Hayes Volcano northwest of the Kenai Peninsula reduced itself to rubble in seven colossal eruptions over the course of a century. Ash deposits, a common feature of Peninsula geology, show that each eruption produced as much ash as the 1980 eruption of Mount St. Helens in Washington State.

A volcano learning center planned for the Anchor Point-Ninilchik area near Homer will invite visitors to learn the science behind this explosive feature of our extreme geography.

Earthquakes and the tsunamis they spawn are another hazard. Small tremors are regularly felt and ignored, but the largest one of them all brought widespread death and destruction to Seward and other areas of Southcentral Alaska in 1964 (see sidebar).

All these occurrences of nature—from the glacially slow to the tidally rhythmic and the seismically sudden—mean the Kenai Peninsula is constantly being reshaped. In some cases, life at these active extremes can be hazardous. But Peninsula residents, like all Alaskans, have an advantage. Survival-minded and historically self-reliant, they prepare for challenges—climatic, seismic, even catastrophic—that might stop a Lower 48 city in its tracks. ■

First Salmon, First Peoples

Can there really be thousands of fish here? I plunge chest deep into gray saltwater at the Kenai River's mouth, hold out my long net, and join a line of wader-clad dipnetters marching parallel to the shore. I can't see into the silty, opaque water, but I know the salmon are here. Like this region's rich prehistory, the migrating fish are hidden from easy view, discernible only in occasional sparkling flashes.

On the beach, modern Alaskan families of diverse heritage—Native, Russian, Scandinavian, Asian—have laid their catch in proud gleaming rows. Sweet smoke curls from driftwood campfires, and the aroma of charred salmon taunts those of us who haven't yet caught our own. Children sprint after their parents. Grandparents occupy folding chairs, gleaming knives and chopping blocks at the ready. Suddenly I feel a light tug. I haul my dipnet back toward shore and there, flopping in the net, is a fat, silver fish. There is barely time to untangle it before other dipnetters back up behind me, looking for sandy space to land their own catches.

Upriver, where the waters run clearer and the angling gear is fancier, fish are often considered sport. But here at the river's broad

*A Kenai woman displays
her dipnet catch of red salmon.*

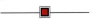

© Greg Daniels

DE LAGUNA'S MAGIC LAMP

FREDERICA DE LAGUNA—Freddy for short—was only 23 when, in 1930, she laid the foundation for the study of Kenai Peninsula prehistory. This archaeologist from Pennsylvania was a Ph.D. student at Columbia University in New York when she became intrigued by five mysterious stone lamps that had been found in Alaska. One of the lamps included a carving of a human head in the bowl. The head would have appeared to float above the oil, praying or gazing at the flame when the lamp was filled.

Eskimos were known for using oval stone lamps, but these unusual artifacts were found in present-day Dena'ina Indian territory. Hoping to solve the mystery, de Laguna headed north to Alaska.

She spent two summers traveling the coast of Cook Inlet, Kachemak Bay, and Prince William Sound, seeking evidence of the culture that had produced the haunting lamps. Some digs were fruitless. The young adventurer endured dangerous Cook Inlet tides, storms and seasickness, constant rain and mosquitoes, and exhausting physical labor. She reflected, "An archaeologist in this country, I thought, had to have the prospector's unquenchable faith of striking it rich the next time, as well as the endurance to suffer disappointment and try again."

Finally, in Kachemak Bay, de Laguna struck archaeological pay dirt. At Cottonwood Creek, on the bay's north shore, she found part of an enormous ceremonial lamp, as well as grave sites. Farther south, at Yukon Island, she unearthed a nearly bottomless midden of artifacts,

---

mouth, salmon represent something more ancient and essential: food. Enough to last all winter long.

Standing deep in the cool water, surrounded by the smells and sounds of fish camp life, it's easy to imagine how the Kenai Peninsula became a cultural crossroads after the last ice age loosened its glacial grip. Salmon, shellfish, and marine mammals lured the region's first people here as early as 8,000 to 10,000 years ago. Successive waves of immigrants representing all of Alaska's Native groups—Eskimo, Aleut, and Indian—followed, interacting with and displacing each other in ways that archaeologists are only beginning to decipher.

Stone lamp, about 1,000 years old.

including ulus, labrets, notched stones, slate mirrors, personal ornaments, and more lamps.

Excavation over the next several years revealed distinct layers of human habitation, now called Kachemak Traditions I–IV. Only the top layer revealed a recent Indian culture. The deeper layers, stretching as far back in time as 2000 B.C., proved de Laguna's hypothesis: that waves of Eskimo peoples had dominated the Kenai Peninsula to a far greater extent than previously known. Though each cultural wave eventually moved on or was displaced, new peoples always managed to find this fertile shore.

A Pacific Eskimo culture inhabited the Kenai Peninsula and Prince William Sound coasts at least 5,000 years ago. In Kachemak Bay, near Homer, archaeologists have discovered flaked tools called microblades, burins, and gravers from that time period. For the next 2,000 years, distinct groups of coastal hunters continued to use the bay as a seasonal camping site. Members of what is known as the Ocean Bay culture, they left behind notch-shaped blades of slate, possibly used to hunt whales, sea lions, or seals.

About 3,000 years ago, people of a newer Eskimo culture—the Kachemak Tradition—spread north and east from Kodiak Island or the Alaska Peninsula to Kachemak Bay and the Kenai River. These coastal immigrants persisted in the region for about two millennia, hunting for marine mammals and fishing for salmon. They left behind great middens—refuse piles—of shells, bones, and artifacts. The largest, at Yukon Island, is 15 feet thick. The Kachemak Tradition people may have painted the ochre pictographs of kayaks, whales, and human-like figures found at several sites in Kachemak Bay. Although apparently successful, this culture seems to have disappeared abruptly between A.D. 500 and 900.

Sometime in the last 700 to 1,000 years, the flow of Eskimo culture from the southwest was met head-on by a stream of versatile hunter-fishers from the north. The Dena'ina Athabascan Indians came, settling along the shores of Cook Inlet, where they applied their inland knowledge to this rich, new coastal environment.

They borrowed the kayak and umiak designs of their Eskimo neighbors, with whom they traded and often warred. They coined words, relying on metaphor and wit to make sense of the new and

A NATIVE NAME PREVAILS

NANWALEK MAY BE ISOLATED from the rest of the Kenai Peninsula, but it sits at the crossroads of many cultures and received 18th-century visits from British explorers and Russian colonizers. Nanwalek was first used seasonally, as an Alutiiq summer fish camp. Then Russian traders arrived. They founded Alaska's first European settlement here in 1786 and called it Alexandrovsk. Other Russian names were occasionally substituted over the years, including Odinochka, or "person living in solitude."

Alexandrovsk was the best-known name for the village until 1909. In that year, U.S. surveyors visited the area and mistakenly labeled the town English Bay—actually the name that British explorer Nathaniel Portlock had adopted for the deep bay just to the north. Finally, in 1992, villagers voted to shed both English and Russian nomenclature in favor of the village's original Native name, Nanwalek.

History had come full circle, and this sandspit-sheltered outpost southwest of Seldovia became simply "place by a lagoon" once again. ◼

the unfamiliar. The butter clam they named *chuq'ush*—"flared or gutted beaver carcass."

In some ways, though, the Indian newcomers kept their own traditions, like traveling light. And like cremating their dead instead of burying them. They showed their respect to the animals they ate by burning the remains or returning bones to the river or sea. If the area's first Athabascan settlers had been less frugal or less clean, we'd understand more about them than we do.

In Kenai and neighboring villages, the Dena'ina Athabascans lived in *barabaras*—partially subterranean dwellings with log and earth walls, covered with roofs of bark and wood shavings. Scant traces of the *barabara* depressions are still visible along the shore of the Kenai River's mouth.

Ultimately the Athabascans spread into Kachemak Bay as far south as Seldovia—itself a melting-pot town—leaving the outer Kenai coast and Resurrection Bay to the Unegkurmiut, a little-known Pacific Eskimo people. By the time Russian traders arrived in the late 1700s, bringing Aleut slaves with them, the Unegkurmiut were already in decline; one village in the Kenai Fjords was abandoned 200 years ago when an advancing glacier crept within feet of the village. Disease and dislocation reduced their numbers even more.

Today, Seldovia remains a dividing line, with Dena'ina Athabascan culture to the north, and a mixture of Aleut and Alutiiq-Eskimo culture to the south. In the isolated outer coast villages of Nanwalek and Port Graham, where early Russian traders and missionaries relocated and consolidated Aleuts and Alutiiq Eskimos under their control, some residents continue to speak their Native tongue, Sugtestun. Elders in these less accessible villages remember many of their traditional ways. They tell stories about Bigfoot, a monster believed to steal children and lurk among the spruce-forest shadows. They relish delicacies like smoked seal intestine and giant gumboot chitons, pried off tidal boulders.

Twenty-five years ago, the Cook Inlet Historic Sites Project identified more than 200 mostly unstudied sites, from *barabara* depressions to shell middens and petroglyphs, on the Kenai

This painting by Belmore Browne depicts early seal hunters.

Peninsula and surrounding areas. Kachemak Bay continues to attract scholars and spawn new findings. In the glacier-scoured Kenai Fjords, centuries-old artifacts show that early Eskimo peoples once found their way among the mist and ice, even though no settlements remain today. Farther inland, archaeologists are busy excavating prehistoric house sites along the Russian River—another salmon fishing hot-spot used by Athabascans, and Eskimos before them—where artifacts hint at continuous occupation dating back thousands of years.

The food resources that lured so many peoples to this land long ago continue to help some modern Kenai residents reconnect to their roots. Of the Peninsula's approximately 3,000 Native residents, 800 are Kenaitze—a Dena'ina Athabascan tribe that, until recently, was one of the most invisible and assimilated of all Alaskan tribes. Perhaps more than any other Native group on the Peninsula, the Kenaitze have struggled to regain their traditional ways after two centuries of intermarriage with Russians and other settlers.

Kenaitze leaders have started spirit camps for their children, built interpretive trails on the Peninsula, and held classes in net mending and other subsistence skills. The late Peter Kalifornsky, the last Kenaitze who could speak the local Dena'ina dialect fluently, labored in the last years of his life to preserve the language and legends of his people. The Kenaitze tribe is battling to safeguard its right to traditional fisheries near the Kenai River's mouth. Catching and tasting the summer's first salmon, Kenaitze children reconnect with their ancestors, one group among many peoples attracted by the resources of these rich shores. ■

First Salmon, First Peoples

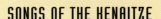

SONGS OF THE KENAITZE

SONGS HAVE ALWAYS BEEN an important part of Dena'ina Athabascan culture. Songs could be owned, sold, or shared; they could even be rented from their proprietors. Ethnographer Cornelius Osgood reported that the Kenaitze, a Dena'ina tribe, had songs to make a man wealthy or to keep children safe, songs for hunting or mourning, and songs to be sung by a husband whose wife was threatening to leave him. And there were songs written specifically for the traditional Native gathering known as the potlatch.

Peter Kalifornsky, the last Kenaitze fluent in the Outer Inlet dialect of the Cook Inlet Dena'ina language, was also the last of the great Kenaitze bards. In a piece he wrote, "The Potlatch Song of the Lonely Man," Kalifornsky sang plaintively about being among the last of his people to remember the old ways:

Where else might we be scattered to?
Where are our relatives?
Where are the friends who might come to us with cheer?
Where are our loved ones who might come to us with kindness?

But Kalifornsky didn't spend the final years before his death in 1993 simply lamenting. He recorded original stories and verses, as well as traditional ones remembered from his youth. With linguist James Kari and several elder Dena'ina, he helped develop a written form of the Outer Inlet dialect. He began teaching.

In the final two decades of his life, Kalifornsky found himself surrounded by younger Kenaitzes ready to learn. And so the lonely song he'd written was amended, according to a newspaper account after his death, with a more jubilant final verse:

Our relatives have come back to us, have come back to us.
Our friends with cheer, too, have come back to us,
have come back to us.
Our loved ones with kindness, too, have come back to us,
have come back to us. ■

Kenai History: Fur, Gold, and Oil

The Kenai Peninsula is a microcosm of Alaska not only in its many habitats, but in its history. Everything that attracted explorers, prospectors, and settlers to the far-flung corners of Alaska attracted them here, too: fur, minerals, the hopeful glimmer of new beginnings in a wild frontier. In many cases, if it happened in Alaska, it happened here first. Russians built Alaska's first shipyard here in 1793. Peter Doroshin found gold near Cooper Landing in 1849, decades before Klondike stampeders poured through Skagway. Oil was discovered here first, onshore, in the Swanson River area in 1957, more than a decade before Prudhoe Bay oil made Alaska rich.

But the Kenai's written history begins earlier, with the arrival in 1741 of Danish navigator Vitus Bering, exploring for the Russians. Bering surveyed the Alaska coast and landed briefly at Kayak Island, east of Prince William Sound, claiming it for the Czar. Sailing a slightly different course, Russia's Alexei Chirikov sailed past the Kenai Peninsula that same summer. On their return, both men's crews gushed not about the beauty of this new *Bolshaya Zemlya* (or "Great Land"), but about the abundant sea otters dwelling along its shores.

Steve Melchin with his domesticated moose in Seward, Alaska, 1900.

◄ © Anchorage Museum of History and Art

By the end of the 17th century, Russian *promyshlenniki*, or fur traders, had expanded their influence eastward from Moscow to the farthest edges of Siberia. The traders subjugated indigenous peoples and decimated fur-bearing mammals from the heart of the Old World to the shores of the New. They sold the furs to China for huge sums and expanded Russia's empire in the endless search for new species, new territories, and new slaves to do the work of trapping and spearing.

Soon after Bering's and Chirikov's discoveries, *promyshlenniki* set out for the Aleutian Islands. They enslaved the indigenous population, forcing all men to paddle and hunt sea otters from their three-holed bidarkas while a Russian overseer commandeered the middle seat. Ultimately the Native population of the Aleutians was reduced by more than half; the sea otters were nearly exterminated.

As the Aleutian sea otter went the way of the Siberian sable, the Russians pressed eastward again. In 1778, when the British explorer James Cook made contact with Dena'ina Indians along the Kenai Peninsula coast, the Dena'ina already possessed Russian trading beads. The Russians began hunting Cook Inlet sea otters in the 1780s, taking more than 3,000 skins each year. The Kenaitze Dena'ina, like the Aleutian Natives, were taken hostage and forced to hunt and conduct trade for their gun-wielding masters.

In 1786, Grigorii Shelikov started a small fur trading post at Alexandrovsk (now Nanwalek)—the first European settlement on the Alaska mainland. Alexander Baranov, the moody and ambitious Russian-American Company manager who succeeded Shelikov, fortified an alliance with the Kenaitze by agreeing to marry the chief's beautiful 18-year-old daughter, Anna. He already had a wife back home in Russia.

Baranov oversaw construction of Alaska's first shipyard—in Resurrection Bay, at modern-day Seward. The shipyard and settlement, Baranov argued, would keep a rival fur company from expanding into nearby Prince William Sound. Construction of the frigate *Phoenix* was completed at the shipyard in 1794, despite great difficulties—insufficient timber, almost no nails or iron or pitch when work began, and an attempt on Baranov's life by his disgruntled laborers.

KENAI HISTORY: FUR, GOLD, AND OIL

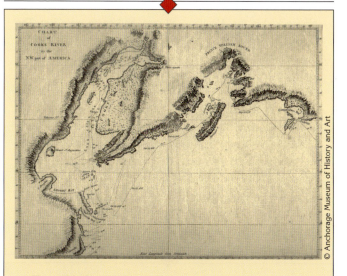

This 1784 "Chart of Cook's River," as Cook Inlet was formerly called, is one of that period's best-detailed.

HIDDEN TREASURE

BRITISH CAPTAIN JAMES COOK sailed into Cook Inlet in May 1778, claiming it for England—although Russians and Spaniards were already hoisting flags in the same region. On June 1, Cook's two ships anchored off what is now called Point Possession, at the northern tip of the Kenai Peninsula. The vessels looked like "giant bird[s] with great white wings," according to one Native account,

A party led by Lt. James King went ashore. Forty Natives watched as the Europeans displayed a flag and buried a bottle of coins, signifying a claim to the land. Incidentally, a local dog bit the ship's surgeon. To display their firearms, Cook's men shot the dog.

Several aspects of the story, including the shooting of the dog, survive in oral accounts by Dena'ina Indians of the Point Possession area. Children raised on the lore of the buried bottle search for it, still. ■

Just five years after it was launched, the *Phoenix* was shipwrecked in the Aleutians; all crew and cargo were lost. The shipyard produced no more vessels. The *Phoenix* and its short-lived shipyard epitomize Russian trading history on the Kenai Peninsula: brief, difficult, and brutal.

Peninsula Natives suffered at the hands of the Russians, and some fought back. Baranov wrote, "Our establishments on the gulf of Kenai [Cook Inlet] have been broken up three times, and a conspiracy has been discovered to destroy all places occupied by Russians, and to kill them as well as the natives of Kadiak [Kodiak] in their employ; and we have not been able as yet entirely to suppress the spirit of rebellion."

No spirit could save the Dena'ina from the toll of disease, which struck hard in 1838. Russian missionaries started a

AFTER THE RUSSIANS

Although Russia's great fur-hunting fleets left the Kenai Peninsula for lands east and south during the first part of the 19th century, Russian influence remained. One group of retired Russian-American Company workers, many of whom had married Native women, decided against returning to their motherland and started an agricultural colony at modern-day Ninilchik.

Even more lasting was the Russian Orthodox faith. Though some observers predicted the faith would vanish when the United States purchased Alaska in 1867, many Peninsula Natives embrace Russian Orthodox icons and dogma even today. Onion domes still reach skyward in several Peninsula communities. Built in 1896, the Holy Assumption of the Virgin Mary Russian Orthodox Church in the town of Kenai is one of Alaska's oldest Russian Orthodox churches. The colorful and icon-filled Russian Orthodox church in Ninilchik, built in 1901, also welcomes visitors.

The sea otter, prey of the Russian hunters, similarly endured. Though a government surveyor reported the otter "nearly exterminated" as recently as 1918, the feisty and gregarious mammal has reclaimed its former domain after many decades of protection.

Kenai History: Fur, Gold, and Oil

Tustumena Lake hunters load a moose into their boat, in the days before creation of the Kenai National Wildlife Refuge.

---

vaccination program against the smallpox, but only one-third of approximately 3,000 Dena'ina survived. By this time, Cook Inlet otters had been hunted to near extinction, and the tide of colonization had moved onward. Many of the Russians had followed Baranov to Sitka in southeastern Alaska, where he established the new capital of Russian America.

As the fur boom drew to a close, the search for quick riches headed landward. For over a century, prospectors and entrepreneurs of all kinds hiked, mushed, sailed, and rowed through Kenai wilderness, searching for gold, or struggling to profitably mine coal, chromite, lime, and other exportable minerals. Some settled and stayed. Many more departed after a few years with scant profits and little glory, but lots of adventuresome tales.

Even prospectors' unsuccessful ventures—and there were many—shaped the Peninsula's future, with the possibility of great wealth "furnishing a lure which led them over mountain ranges and up every river and stream tributary," in the words of Kenai mining historian Mary J. Barry.

HIKING IN GOLD COUNTRY

*Fall colors make autumn glorious
on the Resurrection Pass Trail.*

IT'S EARLY SEPTEMBER and we're kicking through piles of gold. Yellow aspen leaves, really—but we're happy pretending. My young son and I head north from the Resurrection Pass trailhead in a delirium, like prospectors who have struck it rich.

After all, it's autumn in Alaska—not too early for snow at these altitudes—and we have lucked out. The sky is a brilliant blue. Golden sunlight filters through the trees. Between piles of leaves, the forest floor blazes red, all the low berry shrubs painted fall colors.

Our plan today is to hike as far as we can, hoping to rendezvous with my husband, who has been heading south from the Hope trailhead for several days. If his 38-mile hike and our 2-mile ramble coincide, we should meet up shortly. Except for one problem. Berries. Everywhere. We'd keep walking, but we can't stop picking. The tiniest jewel-like cranberries grow in dense mats along the trail's edge, while summer's last batch of dusky blueberries hang from dew-covered bushes. We fill every bag we've brought.

On this day, we get the trail all to ourselves. But on other weekends, the Resurrection Pass Trail hums with traffic— about 10,000 hikers, mountain bikers, hunters, and skiers use it each year. The trail between Cooper Landing and Hope climbs from forest to tundra and back down again, offering glimpses of dozens of small creeks and secluded trout lakes. There's history along the route, too. About half of the prospectors who flooded into Hope and Sunrise at the turn of the century used this overland route. Many of them found only disappointment, discovering nothing but traces of "color" in their search for gold.

But on a crisp, bug-free day like this, I like to believe that among those thousands of unrewarded prospectors were a few who, for at least one shining moment, appreciated the natural beauty surrounding them. Perhaps they got a little giddy. Maybe the delirium was infectious. Maybe that's why one prospector claimed all the water in Sixmile Creek. Or why another blazed a tree and left this note attached: "I hereby claim 1,300 feet straight up in the air!" On a gorgeous fall day, when there's more gold overhead than anywhere else, why not? ■

Goldpanners swirl and hope at Bear Creek, in the Resurrection River drainage, 1916. (Leigh Hill French Collection)

Unrewarded quests nonetheless filled maps and carved trails. But here, as elsewhere in Alaska, the search was never easy. Barry wrote, "Darwin couldn't have proposed a setting more suitable for weeding out the weak, dependent, easily discouraged or purely unlucky individuals than the early-day gold fields of Alaska."

Peter Doroshin is credited as the Kenai's first successful gold-seeker. Working for the Russian-American Company, he spent two years finding traces of "color" nearly everywhere he looked, in the Kenai River and some of its tributaries. But his employers weren't impressed by the scattered ounces he managed to collect. In 1852 they redirected him toward a search for coal.

On Doroshin's suggestion, the Russians opened a coal mine at Port Graham, where British explorer Nathaniel Portlock had first noted coal seams 70 years earlier. Ultimately unprofitable, Alaska's earliest coal mine operated until 1867. Later visitors reported seeing shackles among the mining ruins, suggesting that some laborers, including Native recruits, didn't toil voluntarily.

Kenai History: Fur, Gold, and Oil

Many later companies operated short-term coal ventures, and the Homer Spit in Kachemak Bay was once called Coal Spit. The name Kachemak Bay has been interpreted as meaning "smoky bay," an Aleut reference to smoldering coal seams in the rust-colored bluffs framing the bay.

The town of Homer was named after gold miner Homer Pennock, who arrived in 1896 on board the *Excelsior* with a crew of 52 prospectors. But Homer got its real start four years later, when the Cook Inlet Coal Fields Company built a dock and more than 7 miles of railroad track connecting the Homer Spit to the hillside coal mines. The operation did not last long. Cook Inlet Coal Fields closed in 1902, leaving Homer a ghost town until its gradual rebirth more than a decade later.

Boom-and-bust was the norm all over the Peninsula at the turn of the 20th century, and the biggest boom of all happened along the shores of Turnagain Arm, in two towns whose names say it all: Hope and Sunrise. Since Peter Doroshin's day, Russians had continued to mine modest amounts of gold throughout the Kenai. Finally, Americans joined the action. In 1888 a loner named Al King rowed a rotting dory up treacherous Turnagain Arm and disappeared into the forest near modern-day Hope. He wasn't seen again for a year and a half. But when he appeared at a trading post in Kenai, ready to pay back a grubstake debt, he was carrying four pokes of gold.

King's gold lured other Cook Inlet prospectors, who staked claims on Sixmile and Resurrection Creeks. Tents and log cabins

COAL FOR THE TAKING

Coal outcroppings dot bluffs around much of the lower Kenai Peninsula. An estimated 400 million tons of coal deposits are in the vicinity of Homer. From ancient times to present, people have strolled, mushed, or motored along the beaches, pocketing lumps to burn. Even today, wintertime Homer smells faintly of acrid, smoky coal—a free source of fuel for people living the simple life at the end of the road. ■

sprang up in Hope and nearby Sunrise. The sluicing season was short—60 to 90 days, with late-lingering snows, floods, and bloodthirsty mosquitoes adding to miners' distress. "I would not advise anyone to come here with the expectation of finding anything fabulously rich," one miner wrote to friends in 1895. But some folks did succeed.

When word reached Seattle that one party had extracted gold worth $40,000 in a few months, the stampede was on. The next year, 3,000 miners stormed through the Turnagain Arm District and surrounding areas. Most didn't stay long. Modest riches for hard work paled next to the lure of even bigger stampedes like the Yukon's Klondike. In all, the Turnagain District yielded about $1 million in gold between 1895 and 1906. Then Sunrise became a ghost town, and Hope all but emptied out.

Meanwhile, gold-rush prosperity convinced Alaskans they needed better transportation to link ice-free ports in the south with the growing Interior. Many rail lines were proposed, but Seward won out. In 1923, nearly 20 years after construction began, President Warren Harding arrived to tap the final "golden spike," commemorating completion of the Alaska Railroad line from Seward to Fairbanks. The Seward newspaper honored the occasion by naming the ice field west of town after Harding.

For two centuries, dreams of quick, extractable wealth had led the exploration and settlement of the Kenai Peninsula. But as time passed, a different breed of adventurer began to come north, looking for wilderness to be enjoyed, rather than mined or developed.

Renowned artist-illustrator Rockwell Kent, who visited Fox Island near Seward for a year with his 9-year-old son, was an early refuge-seeker who found bliss on the Kenai. "At the first softening of the coast toward a cove or inlet," he wrote in 1918, "you imagine all the mild beauties of a safe harbor, the quiet water and the beach to land upon, the house-site, a homestead of your own, cleared land, and pastures looking seaward."

Many who, like Kent, fell in love with the countryside did whatever they could to survive and stay put. People tried their hand at herring fishing, salmon canning, and fox farming. The climate

Kenai History: Fur, Gold, and Oil

A Seward settler proudly displays his crops.

was too harsh to allow large-scale agricultural farming, but the long days of summer did yield basketball-sized cabbages, turnips, and grassy pastures.

The end of War World II brought an influx of homesteaders eager to own a tranquil corner of the Kenai. Soldotna was founded

A canoeist fly-fishes away from the crowds.

in 1947 by veterans, who were granted a 90-day preference over non-veterans. To lay claim to their 40- to 160-acre parcels, some boated to Kenai and tramped 11 miles east to Soldotna, while others took the rails from Seward to Moose Pass, and then faced a longer 70-mile trek west.

Once settled, families endured isolation and a daily struggle against the elements. Just getting from place to place was a challenge: The extension of the Sterling Highway from Kenai to Homer wasn't completed until 1950. Sometimes one family member would work an industrial job far away in bustling Anchorage to save enough cash to build the next addition to a simple backwoods home.

Then suddenly, in 1957, it stopped being necessary to go so far to find high-paying work. Oil was discovered in the Swanson Oil Field, on the Peninsula's northwest flatlands. The north Kenai—and Alaska, which gained statehood two years later—raced into the modern age. Offshore production in upper Cook Inlet began in the late 1960s. Local construction skyrocketed and residents prospered. In this one corner of the Peninsula at least, mini-malls, trailer parks, and car dealerships sprouted where muskeg and pristine streams had formerly predominated, and plenty of old-timers didn't care much for the change.

Environmental concerns were magnified by the 1989 *Exxon Valdez* oil spill in nearby Prince William Sound, which darkened shores along the outer Kenai coast and into Kachemak Bay. Now, Peninsula residents question not only the possibility of oil spills, but the production of everyday processing wastes that get pumped back into Cook Inlet from offshore platforms.

In 1960 the Peninsula had about 9,000 residents. Since then, the population has increased more than fivefold, to 46,000. But even with such impressive growth, residents still find plenty of room to stretch and breathe. Visitors share Rockwell Kent's zeal for having discovered what is, even today, a relatively unspoiled land. "To sail uncharted waters and follow virgin shores," he wrote. "What a life . . . !" ∎

Flora:
Shaped by Fire and Ice

One hot afternoon on the central Peninsula's Hidden Creek Trail, we feel like we're walking along the back of a mangy old dog. The spruce trees here are skinny and coal-black, blistered by a 1996 fire that consumed 5,200 acres. The air is dry; sun beats down on our heads. Even grasses growing alongside the trail bend in defeat. But rounding a rocky hill—one of the dog's knobby vertebrae—we are greeted by a fresh breeze and an explosion of pink. Flowered spikes of the fireweed plant blanket these charred hills, a testament to regeneration.

The fireweed's fuchsia flowers deserve a special place in Kenai hearts for two reasons. First, the plant symbolizes Alaska's short, intense summers. Folk wisdom says that summer begins when the blossoms on the bottom part of the stem open. When the top blossoms open, eight weeks or so later, summer is on its way out.

But fireweed has another meaning here in this dynamic landscape, a place shaped by fire and ice. The plant is "a badge of nature's rural renewal program," writes botanical author Adele Dawson. "No soil is too thin, poor or unlikely for fireweed." Fireweed, as its name suggests, thrives in burned areas. Their

Fireweed grows among scorched trees near Skilak Lake.

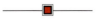

Rust-colored beetle-killed spruce are visible from this Skilak Lake lookout.

---

deep, horizontal roots escape damage inflicted on more fragile plants. They also grow along thin-soiled coastal beaches, on steep hillsides, on gravelly riverbanks, and along the margins of receding glaciers. Fireweed is a pink flag, marking the many spots where the land is changing.

We don't see any moose during this three-hour hike to the shore of Skilak Lake, but we might consider looking again in a few years. Like the fireweed, moose thrive in these burnt forests, browsing on the birch, willow, and aspen saplings that return first. About 5 to 10 years after a hot, widespread burn, local moose populations skyrocket.

Fires are common on the Kenai. A soil surveyor visiting in 1916 noted, "On all the trips we made on Kenai Peninsula, we rarely traveled a distance of more than 2 miles without entering a burned area." Major blazes, natural or human-caused, have been reported at least every 20 years or so since 1890. Eventually the forests regenerate and mature, with spruce trees crowding out the deciduous saplings that moose love best.

Fire is one factor affecting the Kenai's dynamic flora, but there are others. One is so small that it fits on the tip of a pencil; another is larger than a sprawling city. The answers, respectively: the minuscule but influential spruce bark beetle, and glaciers, which cover a tenth of the Peninsula.

Hike inland or kayak along the coast, and you may notice immense, gray and rust-colored stands of dying spruce forest. These trees have fallen prey to North America's largest spruce bark beetle epidemic. The beetles hit hard in the mid-1980s and kept spreading into the 1990s, devastating spruce-dominant areas like Kachemak Bay. Though the infestation has just about

PATTERNS OF GROWTH

THE KENAI PENINSULA'S FLORA is not only dynamic, but it's also diverse. The northern extension of the Pacific coastal forest is found along the Peninsula's eastern and southern coasts. Here the spruce-hemlock forest is lush and wet, a place of mossy streams and gauzy light. Crossing the bay from Homer to Kachemak Bay State Park, you'll notice the south shore's deeper greens, luxuriant ferns, and plump blueberry plants. Near Seldovia, you'll also find salmonberries, bright red and orange edible berries not found on the Homer side.

Elsewhere on the Peninsula, to the north and west, the forest is drier, a combination of spruce trees and deciduous trees, including birch and cottonwood. Quaking aspens paint the hillsides a shimmering yellow each fall. The woodland floor across most of the Peninsula includes dozens of willow species, plus devil's club, cow parsnip, high-bush cranberry, dogwood, and wild rose.

Boggy areas, called muskeg, are stippled by sapling-sized black spruce with an undergrowth of Labrador tea, low-bush cranberry, and other berry plants. Grasses, sedges, and goose tongue wave over the Kenai's marshy areas and mudflats. Wild beach pea sends out its tendrils along the coast and gravelly lakeshores of the Kenai's interior. Tree line ends near 2,000 feet (even lower in some areas). Above this elevation—a large part of the eastern Kenai—stunted evergreen trees, willow, and impenetrable alder give way to open tundra, a delicate landscape of low-growing shrubs and tiny wildflowers. Above 5,000 feet, few plants grow. ■

FLOWERING PLANTS

Pond lily

Behold the Beauty

Yellow pond lily: For me, tranquillity is a shallow Kenai pond, edged by lily pads and these bright yellow flowers. The waters in which they thrive are usually still enough to reflect the sky, and the whole scene—mirrored clouds, waxy green leaves, and floating blossoms—make my heart and hands ache for a canoe paddle. Moose share my fondness for Kenai ponds because of a dietary problem they experience, especially in fall and winter. The woody plants that moose eat most are deficient in sodium and magnesium. Aquatic plants have up to 500 times as much sodium, which is why moose wade with relish, restoring electrolytes as they slurp lilies and pondweed.

Lupine: This plant with purple, pealike flowers is a tough and tolerant species that helps enrich poor soils. It grows along roadsides, on gravel bars, and on slopes. Some Dena'ina tribes used the old, dried seed pods as rattles for their children. Look for it in June and early July.

Other wildflowers commonly seen: Alpine forget-me-not, wild geranium, wild rose, columbine,

Lupine

shooting star, chocolate lily, iris, bluebell, marsh cinquefoil, toadflax, and Jacob's ladder.

Beware the Danger

Devil's club: As ferocious as its name, this member of the ginseng family sports large maple-shaped leaves fringed with spiky hairs, and exceptionally thorny stems. Dense tangles of the plant can make some woodland areas nearly impenetrable. In August a reddish spike of toxic berries ripens atop the plant. Despite its hazardous appearance, devil's club has many medicinal uses. The Dena'ina make a fever-reducing tea from the boiled stems and branches.

Devil's club

Monkshood

Monkshood: Once called wolfbane, this hooded wildflower has been used for killing wolves and coating the ends of darts and spears with poison. It's among Alaska's most lethal plants. The purple flower blooms in July and August, on streambanks, in moist woodlands, and along the coast.

Other hazardous plants commonly seen: cow parsnip (irritates skin); baneberry, water hemlock, and bog rosemary (all poisonous if eaten). ■

run its course, it will continue to transform the Peninsula in years to come as infected trees fall or are removed.

Many homeowners lament the loss of granddaddy spruce trees, and environmentalists question the aggressive salvage logging that boomed in the bark beetle's wake. Cutting large forest areas may reduce fire dangers, but it leaves its own scars: new roads where none existed, and disturbed bear and salmon habitat.

The epidemic isn't all bad news, though. Allowed to proceed naturally, it may even be necessary for long-term forest regeneration. In Homer, grassy meadows with wide-open views of distant glaciers are replacing shadowy, lush forests. Deciduous trees and other conifers, like hemlock, may now get their day in the sun. Dense forest will return someday, but probably with a greater mix of tree species. In any case, the beetle isn't new to the Peninsula. Travel accounts from the 1880s tell of a similar epidemic in the southern part of the Peninsula.

Taking an even longer view, glaciers have reshaped the flora of the Kenai Peninsula for thousands of years. The ice giants have regularly advanced and retreated, carving valleys and plowing under vegetation, and then shrinking back, leaving rocky soils that are slowly recolonized. One of the easiest places to watch this slow rebirth is at Exit Glacier near Seward, where a short interpretive trail leads directly to the glacier's face.

After glacial ice has receded, lichens help rebuild the soil. Then the hardiest recolonizers—fireweed, willow, and alder—set down their roots, just as they do in wildfire-burned and human-disturbed areas. These shrubby plants thrive for several decades, helping to stabilize the soil. They are joined by cottonwood trees, which ultimately tower above the shrubs.

Only when a half-century's leaf litter has enriched the soil, and the cottonwood trees have matured into a shady glen, will spruce saplings rise from the forest floor. For another 50 years, cottonwood, spruce, and sometimes hemlock thrive together. Eventually the landscape matures into a "climax" spruce forest with an understory of mosses, ferns, and berry plants. But the change doesn't end there. When glaciers advance, they'll plow the land again, scraping the forest down to its very bedrock. ■

HOW TO SPEAK TO PLANTS

Blueberries, a timeless harvest.

THE KENAI'S DENA'INA INDIANS, just one branch of the large Athabascan Indian family, have always used the Peninsula as their natural pharmacy. Much lore evolved about the gathering of plants and the hazards of disrespecting nature's bounty.

According to botanical chronicler Priscilla Russell Kari, this was especially true in the mountains, where powerful plants grew and mythical beings known as the *dghili denayi,* or "mountain people," lived.

When harvesting a medicinal alpine plant—geranium, to stop bleeding, or fireweed, to settle an upset stomach—a person was supposed to speak correctly to it and also leave behind a gift, such as a thread, match, or bit of tobacco. The *dghili denayi* would create problems for, or even kidnap, someone who ignored this rule.

The Dena'ina also believed in talking respectfully to trees and in cleaning up scraps left by their wood-gathering or plant-harvesting activities. Children were told it was bad luck to eat berries while picking them.

Wildlife of Land and Stream

"Whoa, excuse me," I say, startled by the moose striding behind the outhouse. She pauses, her spindly legs poised to kick or flee, her blond-tipped neck ruff quivering. For a moment, my senses are intensified: I inhale the warm sweet scent of blueberry bushes baking in the morning sun, and I hear the whine of insects circling the moose's suede-colored rump.

I freeze in place—not afraid, but alert and respectful of this 900-pound animal just a few steps away. Though her bulbous nose and bulging eyes might seem comical to a cartoonist, I note only how well her body is suited for survival in this remote valley: long legs to hurdle-step over willow shrubs and through thick snow, a powerful shoulder hump and stout chest to muscle over hills. Her large teardrop-shaped nostrils and erect ears twitch at my every breath, as they probably twitch at every sound and smell of bear, wolves, and man. Just when I consider turning to retrieve my camera from the nearby cabin, she decides to be on her way, vanishing stealthily back into the woods.

On the Kenai Peninsula, terrestrial wildlife encounters are frequently brief and surprising: the quiet passing of two species, each intent on its own hunting, gathering, or sightseeing

Mother and baby moose browse in a pond near Turnagain Arm.

© Greg Daniels

A hoary marmot munches wildflowers in Kenai Fjords National Park.

---

adventures. Unlike some regions of Alaska, like tundra-covered Denali National Park, the Kenai is mostly forested. At least on land, wildlife-watching can be tricky here. Look high on a rocky slope, and you may glimpse Dall sheep. Stop alongside an open roadside meadow, where morning frost paints the marsh grasses silver, and you may watch a mother moose and her calf munching their breakfast. But the wolverine or the black bear or the lynx who pass within a few hundred yards will likely do so unnoticed, cloaked in woodland shadows.

They do thrive here, though, and that's a fact worth celebrating. Alaska may be huge and wild, but it's surprisingly fragile. Spawning streams, tundra, coastline close to oil drilling and shipping sites, and any wilderness adjacent to a city are particularly vulnerable. The Kenai is home to all four. That makes it not only Anchorage's backyard, but its wildlife laboratory. Here, people ask: Can brown bears live alongside growing towns? Can riverbanks withstand the erosion caused by battalions of fishermen? Will snow geese and shorebirds always herald the Kenai's long-awaited spring? The answer, in most cases, seems to be yes, but only with prudence and foresight.

DALL SHEEP OR MOUNTAIN GOAT?

You raise your binoculars for a closer look at snow-dotted mountains. But wait—that dot is moving. Is it a sheep—or a goat? Both white-haired and ridge-dwelling, these two mammals are sometimes hard to tell apart.

Male Dall sheep, called rams, have large brown horns that curve in a complete circle by the time the animals are 7 or 8 years old. Female sheep, called ewes, have more slender horns that may appear as mere nubs. A sheep's body is sleek, with a short coat of hair.

Mountain goats are bulkier, with a dense coat of long white hair, a shaggy chin and legs, and dagger-like black horns that stick straight up. The male goats are called billies; the females, nannies. Alpine life can be tough, by the way. Though they may seem to climb effortlessly, elder billies often have missing teeth and scars, suggesting they suffer accidents regularly.

A final clue for wildlife-watchers: Mountain goats are more shy than their similar-looking neighbors. So if a cluster of large, white-haired, horned mammals are rock-hopping overhead, oblivious to roadside photographers, they are probably Dall sheep. ■

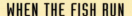

WHEN THE FISH RUN

It's one of the world's most amazing migrations: Salmon that have doubled their weight at sea follow sensory cues upstream, back to the places of their inland birth. All the way home, they dodge fishing hooks, bear claws, and eagle talons. At trip's end, salmon lay their eggs and die, leaving behind the rich organic material that will feed future generations.

Whether you want to wet a line or simply witness this long-distance miracle, head to area streams in season. All of Alaska's five species of salmon—king (also called chinook), red (sockeye), silver (coho), pink (humpback), and chum (dog)—can be found on the Kenai Peninsula. Some top sport fisheries are listed below; consult Department of Fish and Game regulations for specific dates and restrictions.

May: King salmon in Deep Creek, early May; in Kasilof River, Kenai River, and Homer Spit, mid-May; in Anchor River and Ninilchik River, late May.

June: First run of red salmon at Russian River, mid-June to mid-July; kings continue at Kenai River, Kasilof River, Deep Creek, Anchor River, Ninilchik River, and Homer Spit.

July: Second run of kings in Kenai River and Deep Creek; kings continue at Kasilof River and Homer Spit; silver salmon in Kenai River; second run of red salmon at Russian River, mid-July to mid-August; red salmon in Kenai River, mid-July.

August: Silvers continue to run in Kenai River; silvers run in Anchor River, Ninilchik River, and Homer Spit starting early August. ■

Fortunately, that too is a part of the Kenai's hard-won heritage. At the turn of the century, big-game hunters discovered the Kenai, home to the world's biggest moose, plus brown and black bears, mountain goats, Dall sheep, and caribou. National magazines proclaimed the Peninsula the finest big-game destination in the world. In 1900, one hunter noted that the Kenai "has been prolific in animal life but there are so many sportsmen now coming in that the large game is suffering quite a slaughter."

Lawmakers took heed. They fortified hunting requirements in 1908, making the Peninsula the only region of Alaska where licensed guides had to accompany hunters. The action didn't save the caribou, though; the last Kenai caribou was eliminated around 1913.

Big-game hunters weren't the only threat to Kenai wildlife. Frequent forest fires were ignited by careless prospectors and railway workers. Trappers poisoned wolves, eliminating them from the Kenai entirely. A $2 bounty once enticed residents to kill bald eagles. Wildfires and the elimination of predators helped moose numbers soar in the early 1900s, but the population felt hunting pressure as well. A long-term moose decline was noted in the 1930s.

Conservation measures were not far behind. In 1941 President Franklin Roosevelt established the Kenai National Moose Range, a 1.7-million-acre refuge extending from the top of the Kenai Mountains drainage west to the northwestern Kenai lowlands. The range lives on, with a broadened mandate and expanded boundaries, in the form of the 2-million-acre Kenai National Wildlife Refuge.

In recent years, moose have done so well on the Kenai that they have become its fitting symbol. After all, moose signify not just wilderness, but wilderness shared with man. Moose, like humans, are relative newcomers in Alaska. They crossed the Bering Land Bridge from Siberia during the last stage of the Pleistocene Epoch, between 12,000 and 40,000 years ago. It's been theorized that men and moose migrated together, the Ice Age hunters following in the footsteps of their forest-loving prey.

In protecting the Kenai for moose, early land managers succeeded in protecting habitat that now benefits other species as well. Today, following herd transplants by the Department of Fish and Game, caribou call the Kenai home again. The wolves have returned, too. About 20 packs, numbering 200 wolves in all, prowl the Peninsula in search of prey. Moose, one of their favorite meals, number about 8,000.

Other frequently spotted land mammals include marmots, muskrats, coyotes, red foxes, river otters, beavers, snowshoe

BROWN BEARS AT RISK

A brown bear takes a break from fishing.

A HOMEOWNER HEARS THUNDEROUS MAYHEM in his garage: shelves of mason jars shattering, the dull thud of a garbage can overturned. He shoulders a weapon and heads outside to investigate, where he finds not a burglar, but a brown bear. In a moment, the shots have echoed and faded, and the bear sprawls lifeless. Elsewhere on the Peninsula, an armed hiker, backcountry logger, or oil worker is surprised by a brown bear, and reacts with gunfire. Such legal "defense of life and property" kills doubled on the Kenai in the 1990s, to about 8 a year. Habitat destruction and illegal kills have further decreased the bear population. (Legal hunting season has been closed in recent years.) But what difference does one bear make, or two, or three?

A lot, as it turns out. The Kenai Peninsula brown bear population numbers between 250 and 300. That number is small when compared with Alaska's total: 31,000 members of *Ursus arctos*. But it's significant

WILDLIFE OF LAND AND STREAM

when one considers that the entire Lower 48 states are home to fewer than 1,000 brown bears. In fact, Kenai brown bears, a population at risk, share much in common with Lower 48 bears.

The narrow isthmus connecting the Kenai to mainland Alaska keeps this small group isolated from the rest of the state. Like grizzlies in Yellowstone, which face a similarly precarious future, Kenai brown bears are an "island" population. And that small island is shared with an increasing number of humans and an increasing number of land uses: oil and gas development, intense salvage logging due to spruce bark beetle infestation, new road construction and land subdivision, recreation, and tourism.

The Kenai has no official bear-watching sites, and few tourists ever see a brown bear. (Backcountry trails and salmon spawning areas like the Resurrection, Russian, and Kenai Rivers offer the likeliest chances.) But people have had an effect on the bears nonetheless. In the Kenai portion of the Chugach National Forest, one study showed that human activity has reduced habitat effectiveness for brown bears by 70 percent.

Brown bears are especially vulnerable because of their low reproductive rate. Females don't breed until they are 5 or 6. Their litter ranges from 1 to 4 cubs, with 2 the most common number. One-third to one-half of cubs typically die the first year as a result of maulings by other bears, disease, malnutrition, or accidents like drowning. The interval between litters is 3 to 4 years. Consequently, stressed bear populations are slow to rebound.

Since the mid-1980s, several government agencies have cooperatively monitored brown bears on the Kenai. In 1998 the Kenai brown bear was officially designated an "Alaska species of special concern." Conservation groups say there is still time to minimize our effects on this unique population by limiting road-building and restricting human use of key brown bear areas.

The Dena'ina Indians tell a tale about a man and a woman who became brown bears. Other Alaska legends depict the mighty bear as a human ancestor. In these stories, as in modern experience, the fate of man and bear is intertwined. It is still possible for both to enjoy the Kenai wilderness together. ■

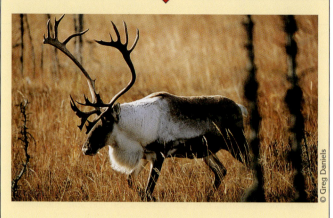

A bull caribou wanders the Kenai.

KENAI'S LITTLE-KNOWN CARIBOU

ALASKA IS KNOWN AS THE LAND where caribou outnumber people. Overhunting at the turn of the century eliminated them from the Kenai Peninsula, however. Antlers from the original herds have been found in remote areas, revealing how extensively these northern nomads once wandered in search of lichens and grasses.

The Department of Fish and Game reintroduced caribou to the Kenai in the 1960s, using animals from Alaska's Nelchina herd to start the Kenai Lowlands and Kenai Mountains herds. The Lowlands herd, the Peninsula's most-photographed caribou, has about 140 animals. In summer they're often seen near the Kenai airport and nearby Warren Ames Bridge. The more elusive Kenai Mountains herd numbers 400 and roams the Hope area, where lucky Resurrection Pass Trail hikers sometimes spot them.

Those two herds are familiar to visitors, but the Kenai also has three newer, flourishing herds that are little-known and rarely seen. Introduced in 1985 and 1986, they are the Fox River herd, with 80 individuals, the Twin Lakes herd, with about 75, and the Killey River herd, 550 strong and growing ahead of expectations. All three newer herds live in hard-to-reach areas away from the road system.

Caribou are Alaska's nomads. Always searching for food, they make long-distance treks each spring and fall, and return to traditional summer areas to calve.

hares, shrews, weasels, voles, little brown bats, and porcupines. There are no reptiles and only one amphibian: the wood frog, which survives Southcentral Alaska's long winters by burying itself under leaves and insulating snow.

Peninsula streams and lakes are home to fish both wild and stocked, including Dolly Varden, rainbow trout, steelhead, and arctic grayling. Along Turnagain Arm, dipnetters harvest eulachon, also known as the candlefish because it is oily enough to burn when dried and fitted with a wick. The Kenai River alone has 27 different fish species. The most prized of these is the king (also called chinook) salmon, a record-setting giant and the official state fish.

Like the Kenai's large land mammals, salmon thrive on the Peninsula not by bountiful accident, but because people labor to safeguard their future. The Kenai is pristine by Lower 48 standards—undammed, cold and clean—but as the state's most heavily fished river, it takes a beating. Riverbank erosion is always a problem. Loss of vegetation disrupts salmon rearing, spawning, and overwintering areas. Many recent projects, including access ladders and riverside walkways, have been built to discourage anglers from further damaging the shore.

As a bastion for wildlife big and small, the Kenai resembles the rest of Alaska. But its proximity to Anchorage and its long history of human use make it different, too. The Kenai offers hard-earned lessons, and also hope. What visitors see as pristine wilderness, the resident knows as a wilderness patchwork—treasured, preserved, and mended. ■

Wildlife of Sea and Sky

From the mist-glazed deck of a tour boat, the Kenai Fjords coast looks forbidding. On this June day, dark clouds scud across the sky. Light rain and ocean spray mingle. The sea itself is steel-gray and cold, only a degree or so above freezing. I huddle next to other raingear-clad tourists, rubber squeaking against rubber, all of us gripping binoculars and cameras.

The landscape alone is worth the trip from Seward, gateway to Kenai Fjords National Park—a natural wonder best visited by boat. Rocky pinnacles and tidewater glaciers glow pearly blue even through a thin veil of fog. It's hard to imagine wildlife thriving in such an austere environment.

Then the mist clears. A sheet of ice tumbles from a glacier, sending up waves. At the fjord's mouth, a cloud of seabirds skims above the frigid, rippling currents. The cold means nothing to them. They delight in the massive icefalls that stir up plankton and fish, an ocean feast. About 200,000 marine birds representing 30 species nest along the glacier-carved fjords in summer.

All Kenai coastal wildlife is similarly adapted to these icy but food-rich conditions. And unlike the Kenai's land-based wildlife, coastal species are often easier to see. Except when submerged, they return to predictable rookeries—resting and feeding areas.

A Steller sea lion defends his haul-out.

© Greg Daniels

The author's son shares a friendly moment with a Halibut Cove seal.

Hundreds of harbor seals can be spotted riding ice floes in the fjords. To them, the ice is far from inhospitable. In June, they haul out on these free-moving islands and give birth to their pups. At an age of 1 month, pups owe half their body weight to fat—protection against the cold of the deep sea, where they can remain for up to 20 minutes at a time.

On the Chiswell Islands, steep scraps of rock at the mouth of Aialik Bay, Steller sea lions haul out on wave-splashed boulders and noisily defend their territories. Steller sea lions, named for naturalist Georg Steller, are the largest of the eared seals. At 1,200 pounds, the average mature male is closer in weight to a young walrus than to its seal cousins.

Though Steller sea lions have been harvested for many purposes—Aleuts relied on them for food, and the Chinese once used their whiskers to clean opium pipes—the decline of their population this century seems more linked to overfishing than overhunting. Pollock—one of Alaska's most aggressively harvested fish resources—constitutes about half of the Steller sea lions' diet. In competing with man for fish, Stellers may be nutritionally stressed, scientists say.

Though Steller sea lions congregate in the thousands on the Kenai Peninsula, their worldwide numbers have plummeted. The western stock of the species has been listed as endangered. In downtown Seward at the Alaska SeaLife Center, just miles from the Stellers' wilderness habitat, visitors can watch captive Steller sea lions dive and feed. Visitors can also talk directly to scientists studying the Steller population problem.

CANARIES OF THE SEA

BELUGA WHALES, a relative of the narwhal, have long been harvested by Alaska Natives. The small white whales migrate near shore in large herds, making them a traditional source of *muktuk* (whale skin and blubber) and oil.

The belugas are sometimes seen pursuing eulachon, a small fish, into Turnagain Arm and the Kenai River. Usually only their whitish-gray backs and blowholes break the water's surface. One population of belugas calls Cook Inlet home. A second, larger population lives in the Bering Sea.

Belugas have been called "canaries of the sea" because they whistle, click, and chirp. But they are canaries in another sense. Since whales are sensitive to toxic chemicals, which accumulate in their dense blubber, a healthy local whale population is a good indicator of clean waters, just as miners' canaries were kept as an indicator of breathable air.

Cook Inlet's beluga population crashed in the 1990s, dropping from about 1,000 at the beginning of the decade to about 350 in 1999. Overharvesting is probably the culprit, scientists say. About 70 belugas were killed each year before hunting was curtailed in 1999. But some environmentalists wonder about the larger picture: Is a changing food supply, oil and gas development, or local pollution also to blame? As with most wildlife questions, the answer may be more complicated than it appears. But most agree that the return of a healthy beluga population will be one sign that Cook Inlet is in balance again. ■

OTTERS AT WORK AND PLAY

RIVER OTTERS AND SEA OTTERS are members of the weasel family. Both exhibit the same gregarious, playful behaviors. On the Kenai, their habitat overlaps, because river otters—also called land otters—frolic in coastal waters and near river mouths as well as farther upstream.

River otters, commonly spotted in the Kenai Fjords, hunt both on land and in the water. Sea otters, on the other hand, avoid land whenever possible; they even give birth afloat. When river otters aren't eating or sleeping, they play. They've been observed wrestling, dunking each other, sliding on mud and ice, and manipulating rocks or sticks. They also whine, growl, and chirp.

At 70 to 90 pounds, sea otters are three to five times heftier than their amphibious cousins. But the heft is not blubber. Unlike other marine mammals, sea otters rely almost entirely on fur to keep them warm. An otter skin has about 650,000 hairs per square inch, making it the best-insulating fur in the world. Sea otters are frisky, too, but often what looks like clowning is nonstop grooming, the key to sea otter survival. If their fur becomes dirty, oily, or matted, it loses its air-trapping and insulating properties.

In 1911, when sea otters received international protection under the Fur Seal Treaty, they numbered fewer than 2,000, but they have reclaimed their northern habitat with astonishing success. Though more than 1,000 sea otter carcasses were found following the *Exxon Valdez* oil spill, this enduring mammal still thrives along most of the Alaska coast, with a population over 100,000.

Sea otter

The Chiswells would be a raucous place even without marine mammals. This cluster of islands is part of the Alaska Maritime National Wildlife Refuge and home to 20 species of seabirds. It's frequently included in daylong boat tours.

Thousands of tufted and horned puffins are the easiest birds to spot in the Chiswells. The "sea parrots," as sailors once called them, have orange feet, bright orange and yellow beaks, white breasts, and clownlike faces. Tufted puffins, the more abundant of the two, nest underground, digging deep burrows with their clawed feet. Horned puffins, which have a distinctive black eye stripe, nest in cliff crevices. Aleuts used the skins of puffins to make parkas.

Also vying for perches on the crowded Chiswells are parakeet auklets, common murres, black-legged kittiwakes, glaucous-winged gulls, and cormorants. Cape Resurrection, the turnaround point for many half-day boat tours, is home to a smaller but equally noisy selection of seabirds. Perched atop steep, volcanic cliffs, 10,000 black-legged kittiwakes pierce the chill air with their shrieks. On the boat ride back to Seward, sea otters frolic between fishing boats—the animals are surprisingly bold despite their close call with extinction less than a century ago.

Another summer day, another boat tour, this time from Homer. The scenery is less extreme—no tidewater glaciers; a greener, gentler shore—but the wildlife is still bountiful. Crossing Kachemak Bay to Seldovia or Halibut Cove, I know I can count on seeing seabirds, maybe porpoises or seals, and my favorite, sea otters. But I try to keep any other expectations in check. After all, we're just one boat on a big ocean. Then, just when I'm ready to hang up my binoculars, a surprise caps the day. It starts as a rounded gray back, with a small fin, parting the water.

"Humpback off the bow," our boat captain calls, decreasing our speed until we bob in place. The engine rumbles low, and people on deck lean over the rails, wishing for just one more sighting. There is a quick dark flash—fin or tail—just yards away. We wait again. Just when people begin to fidget, the water explodes. The humpback whale breaches into the air, flashing its white-striped, accordion-pleated underside at us before crashing back down onto the waves. It repeats the acrobatic display three

DEEP-SEA GIANT

HOMER BILLS ITSELF as the halibut capital of the world, a jumping-off place for dozens of deep-sea charter operations. Charters launch from Anchor Point and Ninilchik, too. Most halibut that are caught weigh between 15 and 20 pounds, but trophy fish over 200 pounds and abyssal goliaths weighing over 400 pounds are sometimes caught as well.

In 1994 two people fishing from a double kayak were pulled around Resurrection Bay by a 196-pound halibut that clamped onto a line they were towing. The startling ride lasted half an hour and ended only when one of the kayakers blasted the fish with a 20-gauge shotgun.

Sound too fishy to be true? The same thing happened to another kayaking angler one year later, in Prince William Sound. He was towed for two hours before ending the halibut's life with a machete.

The largest of all flatfish, halibut have a dark upper side, enabling them to blend in with the ocean floor, and a white or light-gray bottom side. Spawning takes place at the edge of the continental shelf, at depths of 1,200 to 1,800 feet. The larvae spend the first phase of their life as free-floaters, swept along by ocean currents.

Only upon maturity does the fish's left eye join its right eye on the darker, right side of the fish, preparing the halibut for a settled life on its side, looking up from the sea bottom. Alaskans have a long history of savoring halibut. Native Alaskans carved elaborate halibut hooks, designed to bring luck to the fisherman. ◾

---

more times before disappearing again into the deeps, leaving us all giddy from such a close encounter.

Humpback whales migrate each summer to the rich feeding grounds of Alaska from Hawaii, Mexico, and western Pacific Islands. They are commonly spotted on Kenai Fjords or Kachemak Bay tours. The large ventral grooves visible during breaching expand to allow humpbacks to take in large volumes of water. Krill and small fish are strained by the baleen plates in the whale's upper jaw. The remaining water is forced back out. Male humpbacks are best known for their haunting songs: up to 7 hours of patterned, sustained vocalizations that may influence courtship or feeding behaviors.

Orcas also cruise the fjords and are occasionally seen in Resurrection and Kachemak Bays. By studying their distinctive fins and body markings, scientists have identified individuals from both resident and transient pods—groupings of orcas that travel together. Orcas earned the name "killer whale" because many of them hunt other marine mammals, including seals and even whales far larger than themselves. We now know that this aggressive feeding behavior is the trademark of transient pods, while resident pods feed primarily on fish. Since the *Exxon Valdez* oil spill in Prince William Sound, resident pods from that location are spending more time in the Kenai Fjords. Other Kenai Peninsula whales—including minke, sei, fin, and beluga—are also sighted occasionally. Gray whales can be seen in spring, when they migrate along the outer coast and lower Cook Inlet.

One of the Kenai's greatest wildlife migrations can be witnessed without leaving land. Each spring, hundreds of thousands of ducks, geese, and shorebirds use the Alaskan coast as a resting and feeding spot en route to summer breeding

LONG-DISTANCE FISHERS

Many Kenai Peninsula visitors come a long way to fish, but none can rival the arctic tern. Individuals that breed in the Arctic have been found wintering in the Antarctic, a round trip of 25,000 miles. The black-capped bird has pointed wings, a forked tail, gray-white body, and bright red bill and feet. Smaller than gulls, terns are agile fliers and fishers, able to hover over water until they spot their prey. A quick plunge is all that terns will tolerate; they don't swim well and prefer air to water. In midsummer, look for terns at the lake that bears their name, at the junction of the Sterling and Seward Highways. The Tern Lake roadside pullout is also a good place to spot ducks, loons, shorebirds, beavers, river otters, and muskrats, as well as Dall sheep and mountain goats on surrounding mountain slopes.

AN EYE FOR EAGLES

AT THE END OF THE HOMER SPIT, Jean Keene staggers under the weight of a pail, preparing to supply her avian visitors with breakfast. It's a typical scene in some ways—a kind retired lady, a wintry gray morning, and birds. But this being Alaska, where everything seems larger than life, the scene has a few unusual details.

Instead of feeding redpolls and warblers, Keene feeds bald eagles. And instead of hauling seed, the septuagenarian "eagle lady" of Homer drags buckets of donated salmon, glittering with frosty slime. Keene lobs the still-frozen salmon scraps toward the eager birds with a practiced arm, a morning ritual she has perfected over 20 years. Restless birds soar overhead, their 8-foot-wide wingspans casting shadows over the shore. A dozen more patient eagles line up on a driftwood perch, their fierce yellow eyes fixed on their benefactor.

When Keene started feeding the birds of prey, a natural population of about 15 visited the Homer Spit on winter days. Now, between 300 and 600 are attracted by the salmon handouts. The practice of feeding wild eagles has attracted some criticism from nature lovers concerned about the birds' welfare. But over two decades, no biological harm has been noted and no official has ever ordered Keene to quit.

Professional photographers aim cannon-sized telephoto lenses from behind a low wall, while tourists watch the feeding from the comfort of their cars. (Keene asks casual visitors to stay in their vehicles, so the eagles won't become anxious.) The photos taken from Keene's beach regularly appear in calendars, postcards, and national advertisements. Each spring, the eagles disburse, not too spoiled to seek their own fresh-caught salmon after the Peninsula's creeks thaw.

This Homer Spit scene is a treat for winter visitors, but eagles are frequently spotted year-round nearly everywhere on the Kenai Peninsula. At midday, when other species become reclusive, eagles and hawks flaunt their fearlessness, circling overhead as they ride warm air currents. Juvenile bald eagles have brown or mottled head feathers. Adults of both sexes develop the distinct cue-ball coloration—

WILDLIFE OF SEA AND SKY

An eagle takes flight from driftwood along the Homer Spit.

fluffy, bright white head atop a brown-feathered body—that makes them so easy to spot. They frequently nest in large, old cottonwood trees along rivers and streams. Just look for a tangle of twigs and branches—the largest nest structure of any North American bird—between 15 and 200 feet above ground, within swooping distance of plentiful fish.

TIDE POOLS

THE RICHNESS OF ALASKA'S OCEANS carries onto its rock-studded, tide-washed shores. Here you'll find an explosion of color and life that rivals any Kenai resident's garden. The flowers in this case are really anemones, carnivorous marine invertebrates that trap plankton in their translucent, feathery tentacles. Anemones can be white, pink, orange, and brown. Christmas anemones are spotted red and green.

Just as the nearly continuous summer daylight helps Alaska plants grow, the long hours of sun supercharges Alaska's oceans, increasing phytoplankton levels that boost the entire food chain. Among the beneficiaries of this explosion are many other seashore creatures you may spot on trips to Peninsula beaches. Bishop's Beach in Homer and the entire south shore of Kachemak Bay are good places to look, especially near the full and new moon, when tides are lowest. The Center for Alaskan Coastal Studies in Peterson Bay offers tide pool tours.

Sunflower stars, Alaska's largest sea stars, are one of the brightest creatures in the intertidal zone—that horizontal strip of coast that is covered and uncovered twice daily, with the waxing and waning of the tides. Sunflower stars are fleshy and large, with up to 24 brightly colored rays puckered with more than 15,000 tube feet. Sea urchins, sea cucumbers, and sea anemones are also commonly seen. The rarer opalescent nudibranch wears a fringe of orange-tipped spikes and, though only 2 inches long, is a fierce predator of other tide pool creatures.

Sandy shores, like the ones framing most of the western Kenai, offer less color than rocky beaches. But they are the perfect place to find clams, including the glossy and fast-burrowing razor clam. Alaska's top recreational razor clam fishery takes place along a 50-mile stretch of coast between the Kasilof and Anchor Rivers. To take part in this challenging harvest, you'll need a sportfishing license, tide table, shovel or "clam gun," and quick reflexes. Razor clams escape predators vertically, by withdrawing deeper into the sand at a rate of 1 inch per second. ■

*Hundreds of shorebirds soar above
Kachemak Bay waves.*

grounds. The arrival of snow geese heralds the northern Kenai's spring. In April, just as winter is loosening its grip on the Peninsula, the straw-colored marsh flats at the mouth of the Kenai River offer a quick meal to visiting waterfowl, including mallards, teals, wigeons, pintails, sandhill cranes, and the snow geese, whose final destination is Wrangel Island, off Siberia.

Some shorebird species travel up to 20,000 miles a year, and they rely on specific stopovers spaced hundreds of miles apart. Kachemak Bay is one of these critical areas. From late April to mid-May, the Homer Spit turns into a 5-mile-long natural bird-watching platform, with different microhabitats attracting various tiny shorebirds, including thousands of western sandpipers, dunlins, short-billed dowitchers, plovers, surfbirds, and black turnstones. Census takers count an average 4,500 birds visiting the Homer Spit each day in late spring. On the first weekend in May, the town hosts a festival in the migrants' honor.

All summer, thrushes, sparrows, and other songbirds add their music to the Kenai's tundra highlands and spruce-forested lowlands. They become most active at dusk, which at midsummer doesn't arrive until after midnight. Loons, grebes, gulls, and terns bask in the solitude of the Kenai's many small lakes, including those along the Swan Lake and Swanson River Canoe Trails north of Sterling. Other water-loving birds, like harlequin ducks, mergansers, and goldeneyes, ride the currents on swift-flowing streams, including Deep Creek and the Anchor River.

The Communities of Today: Work Hard, Play Hard

"Shelly needs her chainsaw back," an announcer reads over the radio. "Sam says the pipes are frozen. And this last one from Zeke: 'Coming in from Seattle next week; need a boat ride across the bay.'"

These "bush line" broadcasts, repeated throughout the day on the Homer public radio station, are some residents' only way to pass messages to each other. More-modern forms of communication are transforming Alaska, but the frontier remains rustic, and not everyone has joined the electronic revolution. I lived in Homer in 1996 when local service providers battled to be the first to connect the lower Peninsula to the Internet. Yet even in wired towns, plenty of folks still live without phones or home mail delivery.

In "end of the road" Homer, population 4,000, some modern amenities are considered optional. The small newspaper office where I worked had a shower installed so that employees who lived in cabins without plumbing could wash up after they punched in. When the receptionist was late, we knew she was busy tending her dogs or chipping a hole in the stream ice to fill her morning water bucket. Across Kachemak Bay, most people live far off the information superhighway. Not only that, some live without actual streets. Tiny Halibut Cove bills itself as the village "paved with water."

A commercial fisherman catches winks where he can.

This back-to-basics attitude has made the Peninsula a refuge for several self-reliant subcultures. Wearing the modest suits, colorful dresses, and head coverings of their homeland, Russian Old Believers first came to the Anchor Point area in 1968. It was the final, happy leg of a 300-year journey from exile and persecution. Following a split with the Russian Orthodox Church in 1666, various splinters of the Old Believer faith fled to China, Turkey, Brazil, Australia, New Zealand, Oregon, and finally Alaska. Currently about 500 Old Believers live in tight-knit communities at Nikolaevsk and at the marsh-ringed head of Kachemak Bay. They work as commercial fishermen and carpenters, retaining their 17th-century Russian tongue and religious observances.

Most modern-day settlers have moved to the Peninsula fleeing a different form of oppression: urban crowding, pollution and noise, or the tedium of a soft life. People joke that urban Anchorage, to the north, is only "15 minutes from Alaska." The Kenai Peninsula, on the other hand, *is* Alaska.

Residents take pride in a lifestyle with few frills, and fewer rules as well. They do not shy from discomfort, and that extends both to work and play. People frequently hold multiple, seasonal jobs: fishing round-the-clock in summer, selling artwork or clam fritters to tourists in summer, writing or bartending or cabinet-building on the side.

They work hard, and they play hard. As if to keep calluses hardened and the soul primed, they invent new ways to pit themselves against the elements, to suffer merrily. In pursuit of entertainment, they endure frostbite and midnight-sun mania. They climb peaks and cross ice fields. They ride bucking broncos and joust from canoes. Then, if they're lucky, they pay a visit to the neighbor—there's usually at least one—who has not only plumbing, but a hot tub and sauna.

Seward, population 3,000, wins the masochism prize hands-down. In January, visitors join locals doing the Polar Bear Jump-off, a charity fund-raiser. With ocean temperatures near freezing and air temperatures even brisker, people dress up in silly costumes and leap into the aptly named Resurrection Bay for brief, potentially heart-stopping swims. At least they have the good sense to have paramedics standing by.

Cabin at Paradise Lake.

A CABIN IN THE COUNTRY

CHOP WOOD, CARRY WATER, STOKE THE FIRE. Sound like your idea of a vacation? The Kenai's early homesteaders toiled for years to build cabins and clear land in the woods. You can indulge that fantasy briefly and cheaply by staying at any of more than 30 public cabins. Incidentally, some of these cabins were erected on the very spots where the Peninsula's earliest trapping cabins once stood. Located on public lands, the newer cabins offer no-frills shelter, plus access to the region's best fishing, hunting, berry-picking, and wildlife-watching, for about $50 or less a night. Reservations are required.

The Forest Service maintains 18 cabins on the Resurrection Pass, Russian Lakes, and Crescent Lakes Trails, plus two fly-in cabins in the Paradise Lakes Valley (reservations: (877) 444-6777).

Alaska State Parks offers newer coastal cabins in Kachemak Bay, a boat ride from Homer, and in Resurrection Bay near Seward ((907) 269-8400).

The National Park Service maintains three cabins in the Kenai Fjords plus a winter-only cabin at Exit Glacier ((907) 224-3175).

Maximum stays are 3 to 7 days. Access varies from easy (a 3-mile hike on a wide gravel trail) to difficult (an all-day hiking or mountain biking trip). Cabins have no plumbing or lighting. You must bring your own bedding, cooking gear, and stove, and bring or gather your own wood. Even without room service, most public cabins are extremely popular; expect to reserve yours up to 6 months in advance.

AROUND THE TOWNS

■ Hope
From Anchorage: 88 miles
What's up: Gold panning, gold-rush history, river rafting.
Now you know: Hope is the gateway to the Resurrection Pass Trail, the Kenai Peninsula's most popular multi-day overland trail.

■ Moose Pass
From Anchorage: 98 miles
What's up: Flightseeing, Summit Lake views.
Now you know: This town was reportedly named in honor of a mighty moose that refused to move out of a mail carrier's way in 1903.

■ Seward
From Anchorage: 127 miles
What's up: Wildlife-viewing boat charters, salmon and halibut fishing, Alaska SeaLife Center, Chugach Heritage Center, Mount Marathon Race and 4th of July celebration, Polar Bear Jumpoff Festival (January), Seward Silver Salmon Derby (August).
Now you know: The $50 million Alaska SeaLife Center was funded mainly by *Exxon Valdez* oil-spill restoration funds.

■ Cooper Landing
From Anchorage: 97 miles
What's up: Russian River and Kenai River salmon fishing, national forest hiking and biking trails, river rafting.
Now you know: A 1990s' survey found this community to be the Kenai Peninsula's happiest.

Seward gives its hardiest fun-lovers six months to recover, then puts them through the ringer again. Each 4th of July, runners pit themselves against Mount Marathon, the 4,603-foot peak flanking Seward. The trail is steep, rocky, and snow-filled. People slide, stumble, and sometimes bleed. The famous race began in 1915, the result of a barroom bet. Competition just to enter the race is fierce, so common is the urge to endure in the name of glory.

■ Sterling

From Anchorage: 135 miles

What's up: Freshwater salmon fishing, access to Kenai National Wildlife Refuge, summer sled-dog tours, Peninsula Winter Games (February).

Now you know: Sterling is the access point to the Kenai Peninsula's most popular canoe trails, the Swan Lake route (60 miles) and the Swanson River route (80 miles).

■ Soldotna

From Anchorage: 145 miles

What's up: Freshwater salmon fishing, golfing, flightseeing, access to Kenai National Wildlife Refuge, Soldotna Progress Days (4th of July).

Now you know: Historians disagree on whether Soldotna was named after the Russian word for "soldier," or for an Indian word meaning "stream fork."

■ Kenai

From Anchorage: 156 miles

What's up: Freshwater salmon fishing, wildlife-watching at the Kenai River mouth, golfing, Peninsula Winter Games (February), Tustumena 200 Sled Dog Race (February), Kenai River Festival (June).

Now you know: Thousands of snow geese can be seen here daily at the peak of their migration, in late April.

■ Ninilchik

From Anchorage: 186 miles

What's up: Clamming, halibut and salmon fishing charters, ➤ ➤ ➤

A hundred years ago, the gold-mining town of Hope attracted settlers willing to gamble. Now, the town of 130 lures adventurers wanting to take a different kind of risk. The Peninsula's best whitewater is found on Sixmile Creek, a stream that offers kayakers and rafters challenging rapids, deep canyons, and waterfalls.

In Soldotna and Kenai, towns with a combined population of 11,000, work centers around oil and fish. So does play. The town of

Around the Towns *continued*

volcano viewing, swimming pool with water slide, Ninilchik Halibut Derby (June to Labor Day), Kenai Peninsula State Fair (August).

Now you know: Ninilchik holds the unofficial trophy halibut record for the landing of a 466-pound halibut.

■ Anchor Point

From Anchorage: 208 miles

What's up: Deep sea and river fishing charters, volcano viewing.

Now you know: The Kenai's westernmost point of land was named by Captain James Cook, who lost an anchor here in 1787.

■ Homer

From Anchorage: 224 miles

What's up: Access to Kachemak Bay State Park, deep sea fishing charters, Pratt Museum, art galleries, Pier One Theater, Homer Spit shops and fishing hole, beachcombing, marine wildlife viewing, flightseeing, Kachemak Bay Shorebird Festival (May), Kachemak Bay Wooden Boat Festival (May), Homer Jackpot Halibut Derby (May through Labor Day).

Now you know: Homer is located in the Peninsula's "banana belt," so called because winter temperatures here are frequently just above freezing.

■ Seldovia

From Anchorage: 240 miles (including boat ride from Homer)

What's up: Sea kayaking, mountain biking, marine wildlife viewing, berry picking, art galleries, salmon and halibut fishing.

Now you know: Seldovia was named after the Russian *Seldevoye*, meaning "herring bay." ■

Kenai hosts a world-class baseball team called the Peninsula Oilers. When residents aren't cheering their team, they spend much of their free time angling, just like the tourists. It can be a painful pastime. The proof is at Soldotna's hospital, where a stuffed fisherman dummy holds all the hooks extracted from anglers, displayed on the unlucky body part that required a trip to the emergency room. Who says people who come to the Kenai aren't tough? ■

WORK HARD, PLAY HARD

WHERE WATER RULES

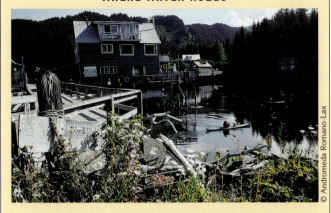

A kayaker visits the boardwalk community of Seldovia.

IT'S HARD TO LIVE IN HALIBUT COVE, population 75, if you're prone to seasickness. Almost everything on this island community revolves around boats. There are no roads to nearby Homer, or in Halibut Cove itself. So most folks jump into their own skiffs for the hourlong ride to pick up mail and buy groceries across the bay. Visitors arrive via water taxi, or they jump aboard the *Danny J*, a yacht that delivers diners to Halibut Cove's single restaurant, the Saltry. The town's sidewalks are really boardwalks, linking the restaurant to scenic outlooks and art galleries, including one that sells octopus-ink prints.

Elsewhere on Kachemak Bay's south shore, water rules as well. Seldovia, population 400, can lay claim to some asphalt. A single out-of-town road winds through the lush spruce forest, dead-ending at Windy Bay on the outer coast. Since the road is frequently washed out, however, a mountain bike makes more sense for visitors than a car. A portion of Seldovia's old boardwalks—survivors of the 1964 earthquake—still line Seldovia Slough. A few bed-and-breakfasts and boathouses, built on piers, teeter above the swelling tide.

Recommended Reading

Barry, Mary J. *A History of Mining on the Kenai Peninsula, Alaska*. Anchorage: MJP Barry, 1997.

Cohen, Stan. *8.6: The Great Alaska Earthquake*. Missoula: Pictorial Histories Publishing Co., 1995.

Cook, Linda, and Frank Norris. *A Stern and Rock-bound Coast: Kenai Fjords Historic Resource Study*. Anchorage: National Park Service Alaska Support Office, 1998.

Field, Carmen, and Conrad Field. *Alaska's Seashore Creatures: A Guide to Selected Marine Invertebrates*. Seattle: Alaska Northwest Books, 1999.

Kari, James, and Alan Boraas, editors. *K'tl'egh'i Sukdu A Dena'ina Legacy: The Collected Writings of Peter Kalifornsky*. Fairbanks: Alaska Native Language Center, University of Alaska Fairbanks, 1991.

Kari, James, and James A. Fall. *Shem Pete's Alaska: The Territory of the Upper Cook Inlet Dena'ina*. Anchorage: The Alaska Native Language Center and the CIRI Foundation, 1987.

Kari, Priscilla Russell. *Tanaina Plantlore: Dena'ina K'et'una*. Anchorage: National Park Service, 1987.

Kent, Rockwell. *Wilderness: A Journal of Quiet Adventure in Alaska*. New Haven, Connecticut: Leete's Island Books, 1920.

Klein, Janet R. *Archaeology of Kachemak Bay, Alaska*. Homer: Kachemak Country Publications, 1995.

Pratt, Verna. *Field Guide to Alaskan Wildflowers*. Anchorage: Alaskakrafts Publishing, 1989.

Quick, Daniel L. *The Kenai Canoe Trails*. Soldotna: Northlite Publishing Co., 1995.

Rennick, Penny, ed. *Alaska's Volcanoes*. Anchorage: Alaska Geographic, 1991.

Rennick, Penny, ed. *Moose, Caribou and Muskox*. Anchorage: Alaska Geographic, 1997.

Schofield, Janice J. *Discovering Wild Plants: Alaska, Western Canada, the Northwest*. Bothell, Washington: Alaska Northwest Books, 1989.

Sherwonit, Bill. *Alaska's Bears: Grizzlies, Black Bears, and Polar Bears*. Seattle: Alaska Northwest Books, 1998.

Simeone, William E. *A History of Alaskan Athapaskans*. Anchorage: Alaska Historical Commission, 1982.

West, George C. *A Birder's Guide to the Kenai Peninsula, Alaska*. Homer: Pratt Museum and Birchside Studios, 1994.

INDEX

*Page numbers in **bold face** indicate photos.*

access, 13
Alaska Maritime National Wildlife Refuge, 77
  Visitor Center, 14
Alaska Railroad, 14, 50
Aleutian Islands, 42
Aleuts, 37
Alexandrovsk, 36, 42
Alutiiq-Eskimo people/culture, 37
Anchor Point, 90
anemones, 82
archaeology, 34–35
arctic terns, 79
Athabascan (Dena'ina) people/culture, 36–37, 38, 39, 42, 44, 58, 59, 61
Augustine Volcano, 31

Babcock, Bill, 25
bald eagles, 80–**81**
barabaras, 37
Baranov, Alexander, 42, 44
Barry, Mary J., 45, 48
Bear Creek, **48**
bears, **68**–69
Begich, Boggs Visitor Center, 14
beluga whales, 75
Bering, Vitus, 41
biking, 18
birds
  arctic terns, 79
  ducks, **26**, 79, 83
  eagles, 80–**81**
  puffins, 77
  seabirds, 77
  shorebirds, 79, **83**
  songbirds, 83
bird-watching, 14, 16
blueberries, **61**
boat tours, 18
Browne, Belmore, 38

cabins, 18, **87**
campgrounds, 17–18
camping, 17–18
canoeing, 17, **52**
Captain Cook State Park, 26
caribou, **70**
Chirikov, Alexei, 41
Chiswell Islands, 74, 77
Chugach National Forest, 15

churches, 44
clams, 82
climate, 13
coal, 48–49
communities, 85–86, 88–91
Cook, James (Captain), 42, 43
Cook Inlet, 22, 23, **30**, **43**, 53
  beluga whale population, 75
Historic Sites Project, 37–38
Cooper Landing, 88
Crescent Lake, **27**
cross-country skiing, 18

Dall sheep, 65
dangerous plants, 59
Dawson, Adele, 55
daylight hours, 13
de Laguna, Frederica, 34–35
Dena'ina Athabascan people/culture, 36–37, 38, 39, 42, 44, 58, 59, 61, 69
devil's club, **59**
dog mushing, 18
Doroshin, Peter, 41, 48
ducks, **26**, 79, 83

eagles, 80–**81**
earthquake, Good Friday, 29
erratics, 26
Eskimo people/cultures, 34–36, 37, 38
Exit Glacier, **6**, 60
Exxon Valdez, 29, 53, 76, 79

fires, 56
fireweed, **54**, 55–56
fish, 71
  halibut, 78
  salmon, **24**, **32**, 66
fishing, **8**, 16–17, **22**, **24**, **52**, **84**
flora, **54**, 55–56
flowering plants, **58–59**
forests, 57, 60
fur trading, 42, 44

geography, 21–31
"ghost trees," **28**, 29
glacial erratics, 26

glaciers, **6**, 25–26, 60
gold, 41, 48–50
goldpanners, **48**
gray whales, 79
Grewingk-Yalik Icefield, 26

halibut, 78
Halibut Cove, **74**, 85, 91
harbor seals, 74
Harding Icefield, 25–26
Hayes Volcano, 31
Hidden Creek Trail, 55–56
high point, 13
highways, 14
  Seward Highway, 14, 15, 26
  Sterling Highway, 14, 15, **19**, 26, 53
hiking, 17, 46–47
history, 41–45, 48-53
hoary marmot, **64**
Hoeman, Vin, 25
Holgate Glacier, **12**
Homer, 49, 85, 90
  precipitation, 13
Homer Spit
  eagles, 80
  shorebirds, 83
Hope, 49–50, 88, 89
horseback riding, 18
humpback whales, 77–79
hunting, 17, **45**, 66–67
  seals, 38

ice fields, 25–26
insects
  spruce bark beetle, 57, 60
invertebrates, 82

Jewel, 25
Johnston, Dave, 25

Kachemak Bay, 23, 35–38, 57, **83**
Kachemak Bay State Park, 15
Kachemak Tradition people, 35–36
Kalifornsky, Peter, 38, 39
Kari, James, 39
Kari, Priscilla Russell, 61
kayaking, 17, **91**
Keene, Jean, 80

93

INDEX

Kenai, 89–90
　Visitors and Cultural Center, 14
Kenai Fjords National Park, **6**, 15, **64**, 73
　Visitor Center, 14
Kenai National Wildlife Refuge, 15, 67
　Canoe Trail System, 17
　Visitor Center, 14
Kenai River, **22**, 23–**24**, **26**
　fish, 71
Kenaitze tribe, 38, 42
　songs, 39
Kent, Rockwell, 50
Kilcher, Yule, 25
King, Al, 49
King, James (Lieutenant), 43
king salmon, **24**

lamps, stone, 34–**35**
languages, Native Alaskan, 37, 38, 39
lily, yellow pond, **58**
location, 13
lupine, **58**

map, **10-11**
marmot, **64**
medicinal plants, 61
Melchin, Steve, **40**
middens, 36
monkshood, **59**
moose, **40**, 56, 58, **62**, 63, 67
Moose Pass, 88
Mount Redoubt, **30**
Mount Spurr, 31
mountain biking, 18
mountain goats, 65
mountaineering, 17
muskeg, 57

Nanwalek, 31, 36, 42
Native Alaskan languages, 37, 38, 39
Native Alaskans, **32**, 33–38, 44
Ninilchik, 44, 89–90
Nuka Bay, **28**
nunataks, 25

Ocean Bay culture, 35
oil, 41, 53
oil spill, 29, 53, 76, 79
Old Believers, 86
orcas, 79

Osgood, Cornelius, 39
otters, 42, 44–45, **76**

paddling, 17
Paradise Lake, **87**
parks, 15
Pennock, Homer, 49
Phoenix, 42, 44
plants, **54**, 55–61
population, 53
Portage Glacier, 25
Portlock, Nathaniel, 36, 48
Prince William Sound, 53
promyshlenniki, 42
prospectors, 45, 47, **48**
public cabins, 18, 87
puffins, 77

rafting, **16**, 17
railroad, 14, 50
Redoubt Volcano, 27
religion
　Old Believers, 86
　Russian Orthodox, 44
Resurrection Pass Trail, **46**–47
river otters, 76
Russian Orthodox religion, 44
Russian River, 23, 24
Russians
　Old Believers, 86
　traders, 37, 41, 42, 44

salmon, **24**, **32**
　runs and species, 66
Sargent Icefield, 26
sea lions, **72**
sea otters, 42, 44–45, **76**
sea stars, 82
seabirds, 77
seals, **74**
　hunting, **38**
Seldovia, 37, 90, **91**
Seward, **40**, 42, 50, **51**, 86, 88
　earthquake's effect on, 29
Seward Highway, 14, 15, 26
Shelikov, Grigorii, 42
shipyard, Alaska's first, 42, 44
shorebirds, 79, **83**
Sixmile Creek, **16**
skiing, cross-country, 18
Skilak Lake, 23, **56**
Skilak Lake Loop Road, 14, 18

snowmachining, 18
Soldotna, 52–53, 89–90
　Visitor Information Center, 14
songbirds, 83
songs, Kenaitze tribe, 39
spruce bark beetle, 57, 60
Steller sea lions, **72**, 74–75
Sterling, 89
Sterling Highway, 14, 15, **19**, 26, 53
stone lamps, 34–**35**
Sunrise, 49–50
Swan Lake Route, 17
Swanson River Route, 17

terns, arctic, 79
tide pools, 82
tours, boat, 18
towns, 85–86, 88-91
trails, 17
　Hidden Creek Trail, 55–56
　Johnson Pass Trail, 17
　Kenai National Wildlife Refuge Canoe Trail System, 17
　Lost Lake Trail, 17
　Primrose Trail, 17
　Resurrection Pass Trail, 17, **46**–47
trees, 57, 60
Truuli Peak, 13, 25
tsunamis, 29, 31
Turnagain Arm, 7, 21–22, 49–50
Tustumena Lake, 25, **45**

Unegkurmiut people, 37

vegetation, 57
visitor centers, 14
volcanoes, 27, 31

whales, 79
　beluga, 75
　gray, 79
　humpback, 77–79
　orca, 79
wildlife
　land and stream, 63–71
　sea and sky, 73–83

yellow pond lily, **58**